THE WISDOM OF TENDERNESS

THE WISDOM
OF TENDERNESS

What Happens When God's Fierce Mercy
Transforms Our Lives

BRENNAN MANNING

HarperSanFrancisco
A Division of HarperCollins*Publishers*

All biblical quotations are from The Jerusalem Bible unless otherwise indicated (Doubleday and Company, New York, 1966).

Portions of this book were published in *The Wisdom of Accepted Tenderness* by Brennan Manning, published by Dimension Books.

HarperCollins books may be purchased for educational, business, or sales promotional use. For information please write: Special Markets Department, HarperCollins Publishers, Inc., 10 East 53rd Street, New York, NY 10022.

Some names and places have been changed in the manuscript to protect the anonymity of the persons involved.

HarperCollins Web site: http://www.harpercollins.com
HarperCollins®, ♛ ®, and HarperSanFrancisco™ are trademarks of HarperCollins Publishers, Inc.

FIRST EDITION

Library of Congress Cataloging-in-Publication Data has been ordered.
  ISBN 0–06–000070–8

02 03 04 05 06 ❖ QUE 10 9 8 7 6 5 4 3 2 1

For the Notorious Sinners who have blessed
my life with their friendship:

John Peter, Paul, Butch, Mike, Fil, Ed, Lou,
Alan, Mickey, Bob, John, Devlin,
Gene, and the other Paul

CONTENTS

ACKNOWLEDGMENTS

I wish to express my deep appreciation for the seminal thinking of Kevin O'Shea and Walter Burghardt, whose insights contributed immeasurably to the writing of this book.

To Steve Hanselman, publisher of Harper San Francisco, who finds "sermons in stories, tongues in trees, books in running brooks," and good in everything I scribble.

To Kathy Reigstad, whose skillful editing made this book more cogent and coherent than the clumsy draft I had submitted.

To my friend Ed Moïse, master chef at the 827½ Toulouse Restaurant in the French Quarter and computer guru whose genius turned the remote possibility of meeting the deadline into reality.

A WORD
BEFORE . . .

In the past year, I've grown increasingly uneasy with the state of contemporary spirituality in the Western world. It has, to put the matter bluntly, the flat flavor of old ice cream and the insipid taste of tame sausage.

Recently, several prominent Christian leaders opined that we're in the midst of a great spiritual awakening, similar to those of the eighteenth and nineteenth centuries. What's one to make of such buoyant optimism? At least this much can be said: when the best-selling Christian books of the past year celebrated self-centered prayer, end-time agitation, and fictitious conversations with God in the green room of Armageddon, we may assert confidently that a national spiritual awakening is not imminent, that silence and solitude are the first casualties of sappy spirituality, and that the superfluity of much useless information and knowledge has been given pride of place over wisdom and personal authenticity.

Biblical wisdom is another matter entirely. In the letters of the apostle Paul, the most powerful prophetic voice in the church of our era, wisdom is personified in the person of Jesus Christ, who is "the power of God and the wisdom of God" (1 Cor. 1:24). This prophetic voice of freedom still proclaims to the contemporary church, "Now this Lord is the Spirit, and where the Spirit of the Lord is, there is freedom" (2 Cor. 3:17). These words are a pure echo of Jesus' teaching: "If you make my word your home, you will indeed be my disciples, you will learn the truth, and the truth will make you free" (John 8:31–32). Why, then, is there so much *unfreedom* in religious circles today? The sad truth is that many Christians fear the responsibility of being free. It's often easier to let others make the decisions or to rely exclusively on the letter of the law. Some men and women want to be slaves.

Wisdom teaches that the goal of our lives is to live with God forever. We're pilgrims passing through, and Jesus counsels us to count how few days we have and thus gain wisdom of the heart. When I accept in the depth of my being that the ultimate accomplishment of my life is *me*—the person I've become and who other persons are because of me—then living in the wisdom of accepted tenderness is not a technique, not a craft, not the Carnegian ploy of how to win friends and influence people, but a way of life, a distinctive and engaged presence to God, other ragamuffins, and myself.

Accepting myself as one loved by God with infinite tenderness, I'm liberated from the vagaries and mindlessness that cling to a potpourri of artifacts and attitudes: the blood line, the nation, the church, money, ego, entitlement, sexual muscle, security, violence, and the paltry gods of modern life. So it is that I reject the "prudence" of church sages from New York to California who tell me, "The love of God is a wonderful theme; just don't push it," and I cling to the God of my experience, whose love beggars belief.

The distortions and caricatures of God that litter today's Christian landscape—ranging from the enraged deity who sanctions the slaughter of innocent cops and firefighters (9/11/01) because he finds abortion and homosexuality intolerable, to the benign, permissive patriarch who winks at adultery, countenances bigotry, and remains unruffled when thousands of hoodwinked Christians finally flee the church to preserve their faith and their sanity—are the handiwork of successful salespeople posing as spiritual leaders.

On the other hand, "When Jesus saw the crowds, he felt sorry for them" (Matt. 9:36). The process of immersing ourselves in the commentaries and lexicons, of dwelling on the profundities of scholars and the reverences of preachers, may have blinded us to the lightning at the heart of this Matthean passage. It speaks of the essential *tenderness* of Jesus, his way of looking at the world, his deepest feelings about us sin-scarred ragamuffins.

If we feel ourselves harassed by busyness, dejected by our unmet needs for affection, and concerned that our lives are a grave disappointment to God, our self-worth may rise or fall, like sails responding to the wind, on the approval or disapproval of others. If we cling to a measure of self-respect, it may be nothing more than what H. L. Mencken describes as the secure feeling that no one, *as yet,* is suspicious.

In the flawed yet powerful film *Apocalypse Now,* Captain Willard (Martin Sheen) receives orders to "terminate with prejudice" Colonel Kurtz (Marlon

Brando), a maverick U.S. Army officer who leads a renegade community in Cambodia. During their first meeting, Kurtz asks the junior officer, "Do you know what freedom is?"

"What is it?"

"Real freedom is freedom from the opinions of others," Kurtz replies, his eyes ablaze with intensity. "Above all, freedom from your opinions about yourself."

We've all learned how difficult it is to dialogue with a person who considers it unthinkable that she might be wrong on any given subject. At some point on the journey we've all encountered people like that. Am I one of them? Are my opinions about myself so irreducibly right that I can't entertain with an open mind a different perception of myself offered by a friend or colleague? Yes, at times I am insufferably stubborn. Are you? More often than I care to remember, I've listened to a person with low self-esteem say something like, "I simply can't accept that Jesus' feelings toward me are different than my own." In other words, the person is saying, "I won't allow Jesus to be Jesus in my life." Such intransigence not only preempts the possibility of living each day in the wisdom of tenderness; it also consigns the speaker to a lonely and loveless existence that disallows Jesus from being the Savior who sets us free from fear of the Father and from dislike of ourselves.

In the experience of warm, caring, affectionate relationships, the heart grows tender. Tenderness doesn't make us more productive; it isn't task-oriented, managerial, or manipulative; it doesn't make us more efficient and doesn't function as a self-help tool to enhance success in the social and financial spheres. The way of tenderness affects our manner of *being* in the world rather than our manner of *doing* in the world. It leads to a gentle presence to ourselves, to others, and to God. It includes an element of self-love, as revealed in Jesus' enjoinder to "Love your neighbor as yourself" (Matt. 22:30), but it's more than that. It includes self-acceptance, but it's more than that as well. It's the feeling that, though I don't have to like myself, I really do; and that, though I don't have to accept myself, I really do.

The Jerusalem Bible is the only translation of the five most widely used (the others being NIV, NAB, NRSV, and KJV) that consistently employs the word *tenderness*. In 1956, the Jerusalem Bible was translated first into French from the Hebrew, Aramaic, and Greek sources;

the English translation then evolved from the French. The French noun *la tendresse* is richer in meaning than the English *tenderness* with which it's generally translated. Used in conjunction with *les bras* ("the arms"), the related verb *étendre* means "to stretch out one's arms" in a gesture of welcoming love. When Jesus says, "Are you tired? Worn out? Burned out on religion? Come to me, get away with me and you'll recover your life" (Matt. 11:28, *The Message*), the poignant image of his outstretched arms conveys longing, intense desire, and a profound understanding of the human condition. Jesus knows that we will experience fatigue along the Way and get bollixed, beat up, and burned out by church, relationships, parenting, ministry, career, appetites, addictions, and our recurring neuroses.

The tenderness of Jesus frees us from embarr? ment about ourselves. He lets us know that we car being known, that our emotions, sexuality, an/ tasies are purified and made whole by his touch, and that we don't have to fear our fe ourselves. The wisdom gleaned from tenderr as ragamuffins entrusted by God, we ca' selves and thereby learn to trust others. V ing tenderness lays hold of our heart?

ever vigilant in protecting itself against pain and seeking only approval and admiration, dissolves in the tender presence of mystery.

Philip Yancey, a self-described "soul survivor" whose faith survived the church, writes, "Although I heard that 'God is love,' the image I got from sermons more resembled an angry, vengeful tyrant." And, he continues,

> We sang, "Red and yellow, black and white, they are precious in God's sight . . . ," but just let one of those red, yellow or black children try entering our church. Bible professors insisted, "We live not under law but under grace," and for the life of me I could not tell much difference between the two states." *

A married priest friend of mine in California sought a letter of laicization from the Roman Catholic

---

* Although I've chosen to forgo the formality of endnotes, each chapter concludes with a list of Recommended Reading that includes works quoted in the chapter, as well as works relevant to the topic addressed. Several titles appear in more than one chapter.

Church that would allow his three adopted children to attend Catholic grade school. He presented himself humbly to the snollygosters* of the Roman offices only to be humiliated. He described the process as "the most demeaning experience of my life." The premeditated humiliations of the oral and written interrogations, directed at a man who had given twenty years of self-less service to the priesthood and who had violated not the gospel of Jesus Christ but a disciplinary law of the Catholic Church, could not and did not shake his faith in Christ and his commitment to the eucharistic community.

When the response letter arrived, it had the acrid smell of a dishonorable discharge. It told my friend that he could never read the Scripture lessons at Mass, give communion to the faithful, or teach in a Catholic institution of higher learning. Furthermore, he had to move geographically from wherever he had last ministered to prevent "scandalizing" the laity (though eighty percent of American Catholics support a married priesthood).

---

* This colorful obsolete word has just been restored by lexicologists to *The New Oxford Dictionary of English*. A snollygoster is a shrewd or unprincipled person.

As Eugene Kennedy, professor emeritus of psychology at Loyola University in Chicago, writes, "Abasement of the other . . . is often the invisible agenda when an inquisitor denigrates the subject of inquiry by the defiling process of the inquiry itself. . . . This is power grotesquely masquerading as authority, degrading its claims to the latter as it systematically degrades those it questions."

One prominent clergyman who was likewise reduced to the lay state (the implicit assumption being that the celibate state is superior) observed, "Catholic convicts on death row have more rights in the Church than I do."

Urged by friends in the past to apply for the same sort of letter, I have refused. I simply cannot, in good conscience, become a quisling—a silent conspirator—in this corrupt and corrupting process. As a Christian, I'm dismayed, infuriated, and heartbroken over its travesty of tenderness. It's an example of why the institutional church, which exists to serve the people of God, is never to be confused with the church as mystery—the Christ-centered, biblically faithful, tender, and compassionate cloud of witnesses who walk the talk.

Of course, church abuse isn't limited to one

denomination. In countless hours of counseling with Christians from a wide spectrum of faith communities, I've heard many stories of people stripped of their dignity, publicly humiliated, and even "shunned" by their congregation. Yet in almost every case their loyalty to Jesus Christ was not only undiminished but was strengthened by sharing in the fellowship of his suffering. These Christians didn't enjoy the pain, but they were enriched by it.

In contrast to the quotidian brutality of the institutional church, Jesus never even asked the adulterous woman brought before him if she was sorry (John 8:1–11). Feeling her abject shame—shame that had been brought on by the merciless interrogation of religious leaders—Jesus forgave her before she even asked for forgiveness!

When preachers and pastors wanting to justify their own fury at New Agers, liberals, provocative clothing, gays, Hollywood, male earrings, and hard rock invoke the manifest anger of Jesus as he cleanses the Temple, they overlook the fact that Christ's anger is the storm-front of his love.

The immense tenderness of the heart of Jesus is touchingly expressed when he visits the town of Nain

(Luke 7:11–17). The only son of a widow has died and is being carried by relatives past the town gate for burial. Seeing the mother's grief-stricken face, Jesus feels sorry for her (JB); he is moved with pity (NAB); he has compassion for her (NRSV); his heart goes out to her (NIV). Jesus takes her face in his hands and whispers, "Shhh, I know." He wipes the tears from her eyes with his thumbs, and then he says, "Don't cry." Jesus is the human face of God, and at this moment (and at every moment), you and I are being seen with the same gaze of infinite tenderness.

To be formed and informed by the wisdom of tenderness has direct bearing on our interpersonal relationships. Illustration:

"You're such a fussbudget!" The irritation in her voice is palpable.

What has provoked this unseemly outburst? I'm simply scrubbing six cereal bowls that have never been used. And I scrub with vigor because, as my mother used to say, if you're going to do something, do it right. Immediately I become aware of two options.

The first is a slashing riposte that will cut her fragile psyche to ribbons: "If, as the great minds say, cleanliness is next to godliness, your shallow, stupid, insignificant soul is sliding into Sheol." The second is, "God help me: I'm obsessive/compulsive when it comes to cleanliness. What a neurotic! I must drive you up the wall. You've been far too patient with me for far too long." Locking my soapy fingers behind my back, I lean forward and kiss her on the cheek, then rest my head on her shoulder.

The heart enveloped in the tenderness of God passes that tenderness around indiscriminately, making no distinction between the worthy and the unworthy.

In my travels these past twenty years, I have crossed denominational lines again and again and been privileged to share the Good News with Southern Baptists and Catholics, Methodists and Moravians, Episcopalians and Presbyterians, Evangelicals and Fundamentalists, Lutherans, Quakers, Anglicans, and Assemblies of God. I'm eager and happy to report that, not only have I met countless individuals who are preserving the Good News of Christianity from the snares of organized religion and the clutches of conventional piety, but I have visited several evangelical outposts—faith communities both large and small—doing the same.

These folks live lives soaked in prayer and centered in Jesus. Flawed like the rest of us, they laugh often and easily at themselves and their pretensions of holiness. They turn their faces toward our broken world with an eye for the homeless and a preferential concern for the poor. At Sunday worship they don't measure success by the number of voices uplifted in praise or the bang-shang-a-lang rhythms of the music ministry. The worship is sincere and joyful, the praise steeped in gratitude. The minister or priest may not be gifted with eloquence, a wide vocabulary, or a charismatic personality, but the quiet fire in his or her belly is unmistakable, and the preaching comes from the heart.

Words without poetry lack passion; words without passion lack persuasion; words without persuasion lack power. When the language of *should* and *must* predominates, both the preached and written word are a barren wasteland void of passion, persuasion, and power. At the close of too many sermons, the exhortation "Now let us . . ." carries neither conviction nor clout. Without the sharing of personal experience, prophetic preaching is impossible. The Word of God must become incarnate in the life of the preacher.

Solitude is the furnace of transformation, and stoking the inner fire is the wisdom of silence. The latter makes speech personal; without it, dialogue is impossible. Words about Jesus that don't come from within are useless, while words born of silence convey intimate, affective, and loving knowledge of the Lord Jesus. In the prophet Hosea, God speaks the way an enchanted young man might woo his beloved: "I am going to lure her and lead her out into the desert; there, I will speak to her heart" (2:16).

Dismiss silence and solitude as trophies reserved for monks and cloistered nuns, and the consequences for discipleship are predictable. The sole criterion for admission to the "kingdom prepared for you since the foundation of the world" (Matt. 25:34) is the confession of Jesus as Lord, not the way "one of the least of my brothers" was fed, clothed, welcomed, and visited. And yet when discrimination against women goes unchallenged; when minorities are considered second-class citizens; when leadership is mastery of mega-church principles and not humble service; when the poor and outcast are not welcome at the table; when obedience to the Father, loving service to others, and simplicity of life are considered the exclusive province of elite believers; when evangelical greatness is measured by achievement and not by smallness; and when

the rejection and suffering inherent in bold witness to
the truth is rationalized, minimized, and finally pulver-
ized in cantankerous Bible studies, then Jesus is made
an anachronism, his teaching an irrelevance, and his
followers an anonymous crowd—their investments and
property intact, their credit cards and trinkets secure; a
sheepish herd moving in lockstep with the lip-serving,
self-absorbed entrepreneurs who stay busy "expanding
their territories to the glory of God."

If we knew the New Testament by heart, if we
heard its thunders sounding in our ears, rinsing them
of the foul sounds and siren enticements of the world,
if we knew by heart one syllable of one word of one
sentence of the Sermon on the Mount, if we attended
to the voice of the eagle of Patmos, if we trusted that
letting ourselves be loved by God is more important
than loving God, never again would we tolerate the
machinations of manipulative religionists who distort
the face of God. Never again would the fallen be publicly humiliated before the congregation. Never again
would distempered preachers be licensed to terrify
people in the pews. Never again would we fawn over
clerical celebrities and bow to the rich and powerful.
Never again would the primacy of loving be subordi-

nated to alleged orthodoxy. Never again would the bar on the pole vault be lowered. Never again would one church dare to malign another, and never again would the prophetic voice of a Martin Luther King Jr. or a Daniel Berrigan be silenced.

The crux of this little book can be stated briefly and succinctly. In a moment of naked honesty, ask yourself, "Do I wholeheartedly trust that God likes me?" (Not *loves* me, because theologically God can't do otherwise.) "And do I trust that God likes me, not after I clean up my act and eliminate every trace of sin, selfishness, dishonesty, and degraded love; not after I develop a disciplined prayer life and spend ten years in Calcutta with Mother Teresa's missionaries; but in this moment, right now, right here, with all my faults and weaknesses?" If you answer without hesitation, "Oh yes, God does like me; in fact, he's very fond of me," you're living in the wisdom of accepted tenderness.

I offer *The Wisdom of Tenderness* as a compass rather than a manual, a beacon rather than a handbook, a vision rather than fifty-six steps to spiritual maturity.

And so, doing the best I can with what I have, I'll try in these pages to share with you my limited

understanding of the wondrous mystery that ragamuffins call "Abba."

A little word. But one that carries a transformative
wisdom beyond all understanding.

Brennan Manning
New Orleans
27 April 2002

Recommended Reading

Kennedy, Eugene. *The Unhealed Wound: The Church and
Human Sexuality.* New York: St. Martin's Press, 2001.

Yancey, Philip. *Soul Survivor: How My Faith Survived the
Church.* New York: Doubleday, 2001.

Chapter One

THE WISDOM
OF TENDERNESS

Every change in the quality of a person's life must grow out of a change in his or her vision of reality. The Christian accepts the Word of Jesus Christ as the master vision of reality. Jesus' Person and teaching shape our understanding of God, the world, other people, and ourselves. This shaping exercises a decisive influence on the Christian's lifestyle.

A simple example: If we accept the revelation of Jesus that God is Father, that there's "one God and Father of all, who is over all, and works through all, and is in all" (Eph. 4:6), then we're making a statement, not just about God but about ourselves. To say, "Abba, Father," in the Spirit is to say that we're children. It's to acknowledge that other people are our brothers and sisters in the human family. This understanding affects our lifestyle because it implies acceptance of others and responsibility for others: we do our best to give family members whatever they need. This familial relationship is to be taken literally, for it's a thing of flesh and blood in the bond of the Holy Spirit. True Christian community is the realization and actualization of "Our Father, who art in heaven."

Classic author A. W. Tozer sees the link between our perception of God and our understanding of humankind as crucial. He writes,

What comes into our minds when we think about God is the most important thing about us. . . . Were we able to extract from any man a complete answer to the question, "What comes into your mind when you think about God?" we might predict with certainty the spiritual future of that man. Were we to know exactly what our most influential religious leaders think of God today, we might be able with some precision to foretell where the church will stand tomorrow.

Formed and informed by the Word of God, saints
and mystics down the centuries have chanted the same
refrain: God can't *not* love us. Without the eternal,
interior generation of love, God would cease to be
God. When we're steeped in selfishness, indifferent to
the poor, tormented by lust, wallowing in self-pity, and
flattened by depression, God's love continues to carry
us. According to John, the essence of our faith lies in
trusting that love of God (1 John 4:16). Salvation happens the moment we accept without reservation what
G. K. Chesterton called the "furious" love of God.
Jesus' life of preaching, teaching, and healing and his
death/resurrection are the supreme manifestations of a
love that defies human comprehension.

Whether your childhood was idyllic or abusive,
the challenge stands: Do you accept yourself as one
utterly loved by God? The human love experienced in
a happy home, though rich and rewarding, isn't even
remotely comparable to divine love, and the absolute
deprivation of human affection isn't an insuperable
impediment to "being seized by the power of a great
affection." Both those who have been loved well and
those who have known nothing but contempt in the

home need stubborn grace to make the leap of faith into the arms of love. Thus, no one is exempt.

But what of God's justice? The Scriptures state unequivocally that God is both lover and judge. Are not the two diametrically opposed? Should not—*must not*—one have priority over the other? Thérèse of Lisieux, recognized as a Doctor of the church because of the truth and depth of her analysis of the spiritual life, penned the following words: "I hope as much from the justice of God as from his mercy. It is because he is just that he is compassionate and full of tenderness." She continues, "for he knows our weakness. He remembers that we are dust. As a father has tenderness for his children, so the Lord has compassion for us. I do not understand souls who have fear of so tender a Friend. . . . What joy to think that God is just, that he takes account of our weaknesses, that he knows perfectly the fragility of our nature."

The genesis of this book can be traced to an extended period of silence and solitude that I spent in the Allegheny Mountains of western Pennsylvania. My retreat began fitfully with several days of physical fatigue, spiritual dryness, boredom, and vague feelings of existential guilt over the prospect that I might be using the ministry to satiate my appetite for approval and recognition. In the late afternoon on the fifth day, I dragged myself to chapel to endure yet another hour of the Great Stare: meditation. As I settled into a straight-back chair, the carillon bells tolled four times.

Thirteen hours later, I rose from the chair and walked out of the chapel with one phrase ringing in my head and pounding in my heart: "Live in the wisdom of accepted tenderness."

Once again, every change in the quality of a Christian's life must grow out of a change in his or her vision of reality. Thirteen hours of silence and solitude radically altered my perception of everything.

If I'm graced to understand with my head and to accept with my heart that the essence of the divine nature is *compassion*, then God is best defined by *the heart of tenderness*. Daily the universal church cries out in morning praise, "In the *tender compassion* of our God the dawn from on high shall break upon us, to shine on those who dwell in darkness and to guide our feet on the road to peace" (Luke 1:78–79, italics mine).

Relating to God as the heart of tenderness identifies the Holy Spirit as the bond of tenderness between

the Father and the Son. Thus, the gentle Spirit dwelling within us is the deepest expression of tenderness—indeed, the Spirit-filled Christian is one whose
heart is overflowing with tenderness—and it represents
the full healing of our pain through his coming to us.

What is the true meaning of tenderness? One must
be careful here: we corrupt our sense of reality by sentimentalizing the concept. When such excess erupts,
the soul is poisoned by romantic emotions and tenderness degenerates into mawkishness.

Noah Webster defines tenderness as sensitivity to
emotions, to the feelings of others. Kahlil Gibran, in
his work *Jesus of Nazareth*, says, "[Jesus'] sadness was
tenderness to those in pain and comradeship to the
lonely." Biblically, tenderness is what follows when
someone reveals to you your own inner beauty, when
you discover your belovedness, when you experience
that you are deeply and sincerely *liked* by someone. If
you communicate to me that you really like me, not just
love me as a brother in Christ, that you take delight in
me (and would, even if I'd never written a single sentence), then you open up to me the possibility of liking
myself. The look of amiable regard in your eyes banishes my fears, and my defense mechanisms (such as

insulation, name-dropping, and giving the impression that I've got it all together) disappear into the nothingness of my non-attention to them. Your warmth withers my self-disdain and allows the possibility of self-esteem. I drop my mask of pretentious piety, stop impersonating Brother Teresa, quit disguising my sanctimonious voice, start to smile at my own frailty, and dare to become more open, sincere, vulnerable, and affectionate with you than I would ever dream of being if I thought you didn't like me. In short, what happens is I grow *tender*.

Several years ago, Edward Farrell of Detroit took his two-week summer vacation to Ireland to celebrate his favorite uncle's eightieth birthday. On the morning of the great day, Ed and his uncle got up before dawn, dressed in silence, and went for a walk along the shores of Lake Killarney. Just as the sun rose, his uncle turned and stared straight at the rising orb. Ed stood beside him for twenty minutes with not a single word exchanged. Then the elderly uncle began to skip along the shoreline, a radiant smile on his face.

After catching up with him, Ed commented, "Uncle Seamus, you look very happy. Do you want to tell me why?"

"Yes, lad," the old man said, tears washing down his face. "You see, the Father is very fond of me. Ah, me Father is so very fond of me."*

Clearly Seamus answered in the affirmative the question posed in the introduction: "Do I wholeheartedly trust that God likes me?" (Not *loves* me, because, as you will recall, God loves by necessity of his nature.) If you too can answer with gut-level honesty, "Oh yes, the Father is very fond of me," there comes a relaxedness and serenity, a compassionate attitude toward yourself in your brokenness, that elucidates the meaning of tenderness.

Could this describe what happened to Jesus at the outset of his ministry? As Luke tells us, "When all the people had been baptized and while Jesus after his own baptism was at prayer, heaven opened and the Holy Spirit descended on him in bodily shape, like a dove. And a voice came from heaven, 'You are my Son, the Beloved; my favor rests on you'" (Luke 3:21–22).

In one of the most dramatic moments in salvation-history, Abba confirmed the unique status of his only-

---

* Farrell, Edward. *The Father Is Fond of Me.* Starruga, PA: Dimension Books, 1978.

begotten Son as the Beloved. For Jesus, the heavenly voice ratified thirty years of growth and searching in Nazareth. It furnished a clear core identity experience: Son, Servant, and Beloved. Abba's favor rested on Jesus as on no other with those words, irrevocably delineating his person and his mission. Dare we suggest that Jesus experienced in the depth of his human soul how much his Father liked him? That Abba revealed his inner beauty to him? Did the Man who was like us in all things but ungratefulness discover his own truth in the light of the loving gaze that rested upon him? As Jesus advanced in wisdom, age, and grace, his baptism in the Jordan River marked a decisive moment in his self-understanding.

And let's not overlook Jesus' ethnic origin. Jesus of Nazareth was a Jew: He was raised and reared in the Jewish culture. His roots were Davidic. Like every devout Jew, he prayed the Shema Israel in the morning and the evening: "Hear, O Israel! The Lord is our God, the Lord alone. Therefore, you shall love the Lord, our God, with all your heart, and with all your soul, and with all your strength" (Deut. 6:4–5). Torah, temple, and synagogue shaped Jesus' interior life, along with the great liturgical feasts—Pesach, Weeks, Sukkoth,

Rosh Hashanah, Yom Kippur—and the whole ambience of Jewish prayer.

Yet there came a point in the evolution of Jesus' religious development when he could no longer call upon God by the traditional Hebrew invocations—Adonai, Elohim, El Shaddai, Yahweh—but had to call him Abba, the very name implying tenderness. Henceforth, for Jesus and for his followers then and through the ages, God had a new name. He would be called Abba because he protects, cares for, understands, forgives, and fusses over his children. Adoration would no longer consist of covering the eyes and face with one's hands but of surrendering oneself with boundless trust into the powerful and tender hands of the One who is forever "Papa."

In his landmark work, *On Being a Christian*, Hans Küng writes,

Abba—like our "Daddy"—is originally a child's word, used however in Jesus' time also as a form of address to their father by grown-up sons and daughters and as an expression of politeness, generally to an older person deserving of respect. But to use this not particularly manly expression of *tenderness* [italics mine], drawn from the child's vocabulary, this commonplace term of politeness, to use this as a form of addressing God, must have struck Jesus' contemporaries as irreverent and offensively familiar, very much as if we were to address God today as "Dad."

For Jesus, this term is no more lacking in respect than it is when used as the child's familiar form of address for her daddy. Familiarity doesn't exclude respect. Reverence remains the basis of Jesus' understanding of God, though it's not all-sufficient. Just as a child addresses his earthly father, so according to Jesus should we address our heavenly Father: reverently, obediently, but above all securely and confidently. To address God as Abba is the boldest and simplest expression of that absolute trust with which we rely on God for all good, with which we entrust ourselves to him.

To live in the wisdom of accepted tenderness is to humbly acknowledge the limitations of the rational, scientific, finite mind and to freely embrace mystery. In the pearl of the parables, Jesus hints at the tenderness of the prodigal father in his response to the wastrel son. "While he was still a long way off, his father saw him and took pity on him. He ran to him, clasped him in his arms and kissed him tenderly" (Luke 15:20). In biblical scholar Frank Montalbano's felicitous translation, we find a slight nuance: "He ran to him, clasped him in his arms and could not stop kissing him; he simply could not stop kissing him."

Whatever translation of the Bible is used, no word can express and no thought can contain the reality of the Father's compassion. As scientists speak in matter-of-fact tones of 100 trillion galaxies bucketing about outer space at incredible speeds, and about the star Upsilon Andromedae blissfully positioned 264 trillion miles from planet earth, we're not surprised that the tenderness of Abba/Creator can't be quantified.

Living in tenderness leads us out of the house of fear. Since the carnage and heartache of September 11, 2001, we've become an increasingly fearful people. Without our conscious awareness, the agenda of the world—the issues and items filling newscasts and newspapers—has become the Christian agenda. Fearful survival questions dominate our consciousness in a way previously unknown. Reticence to fly commercial airlines, to invest in the market, to buy a home or a car, and to make social commitments beyond the immediate future has transformed a lighthearted pilgrim people into a dispirited traveling troupe of brooding Hamlets and trembling soothsayers.

In the face of fear and uncertainty, the faithful remnant—*anawim* in Hebrew, "ragamuffins" in the vernacular—remain agents of hope in what theologian Oscar Cullman calls the "isness of the shall be." The twinkle in their eyes suggests that they possess a higher vision.

Such vision is seen in Peter van Breeman's tale of the journalist who wanted to write a feature story about a particular guru. He went to see the guru and asked, "Are you a genius as some people say?"

"You might say so," answered the guru with a smile.

"And what makes a genius?" asked the intrepid reporter.

"The ability to see."

The journalist was betwixt and between. Scratching his hair with one hand and rubbing his tummy with the other, he muttered, "To see what?"

The guru quietly replied, "The butterfly in a caterpillar, the eagle in an egg, the saint in a selfish person, life in death, unity in separation, God in the human and

the human in God, and suffering as the form in which
the incomprehensibility of God himself appears."*

The wisdom to see the tenderness of God at work
in tribulation and consolation delivers the ragamuffin
from the house of fear, sets her free from the worries,
tensions, and pressures of our torn and tearing world,
and makes the words of Jesus her cry of liberation:
"There is no need to be afraid, little flock, for it has
pleased your Father to give you the Kingdom" (Luke
12:32).

To live in the wisdom of tenderness is to let go of
cares and concerns, to stop organizing means to ends,
and to simply *be* in each moment of awareness as an
end in itself. It's to hear with the heart the word of Paul
to Titus: "The tenderness and love of God our Savior
has dawned in our lives; he saved us not because of any
righteous deeds we had done but because of his mercy"
(3:4–5).

The wisdom of tenderness allows us to love our
whole life story and know that we've been graced and

* Stella, Tom. *The God Instinct.* Notre Dame, IN: Sorin Books,
2001.

made beautiful by the providence of our past history. "Even from my sins," wrote Augustine of Hippo, "God has drawn good." All the wrong turns in the past, the detours, the mistakes, the moral lapses—*everything* that's irrevocably ugly or painful melts and dissolves in the light of accepted tenderness. As Australian theologian Kevin O'Shea remarks, "One rejoices in being unafraid to be open to the healing presence, no matter what one might be or what one might have done."

Perhaps we're not far removed from the experience of Paul: "I give no thought to what lies behind but push on to what lies ahead" (Phil. 3:13). If Paul had dwelt on the gravity of his guilt in the Christian persecutions and the stoning of Stephen (at which Saul apparently held the coats of the assassins—Acts 8:58), he would have gone to his grave bewitched. If Paul hadn't gone through the humble but enlivening experience of divine tenderness, he might well have become pathological. The fourteen epistles would never have been written, the reign of God would not have been extended over the Gentile world (at least through him), and countless believers would have been denied the knowledge he gave us of the mystery of salvation. Paul would have died a guilt-ridden, brokenhearted man. But in the depths of Paul's melancholy, the risen Jesus tenderly led him into graced peacefulness.

Self-hatred for real or imagined failures begets crippling guilt and is spawned by the father of lies. It thwarts God's plan for our existence, our personal standing in the world. When we scorn ourselves and say, "I'm a born loser, a fraud, a hypocrite," then we scorn the divine plan—scorn all the dreams God would realize through us, all the joy he anticipates from us, and all the hope he has placed in us.

The understanding of God's Spirit as the tenderness between the Father and the Son suggests an uncomplicated spirituality tuned in to the present moment in the total simplicity of the here and now ("I give no thought to what lies behind . . ."). To dispatch yesterday's cares and disdain tomorrow's concerns is a strong evangelical imperative. "So do not worry about tomorrow; tomorrow will take care of itself. Each day has enough trouble of its own" (Matt. 6:34).

The meaning of the *here and now* is beautifully illustrated by a Zen story about a monk being pursued by a ferocious tiger. Approaching a precipitous chasm, the monk looked back and saw the tiger about to spring. In the nick of time he saw a rope hanging over the edge of the cliff and began to shimmy down it, out of the clutches of the tiger. Whew! Then he checked below and saw a quarry of huge, jagged rocks. Not so good. Back up, maybe? No, the tiger was poised atop with bared claws. As he weighed his options, two mice began to nibble at the rope.

What to do? The monk saw a strawberry within arm's reach growing out of the face of the cliff. He plucked it, ate it, and pronounced it the best strawberry he had ever tasted. If he had been preoccupied with the rocks below (the future) or with the tiger above (the past), he could have missed the strawberry that God was giving him in the present moment.*

Although only moments from death, the monk feasted on the *here and now*. Life in the Spirit continually sends us tigers and jagged rocks—and strawberries. Do we let ourselves enjoy the strawberries? Or do we squander our diffused consciousness worrying about the dangers of the past and the future?

* Keyes, Ken. *Handbook of Higher Consciousness*. Berkeley, CA: Living Love Center, 1972.

Living in the wisdom of accepted tenderness means receiving each moment as an end in itself. This way of living doesn't demand that we try to be especially recollected in spite of the distractions of work and life. Strained effort to stay centered has been self-defeating, in my personal experience: my work has been sloppy and I've been strung-out. Neither does it advocate efforts to attain a special state of consciousness that might be called "contemplative." In my case, that has led to drowsiness and eventual torpor. Nor does it try to focus on God "up there and out there," independent of our natural contact with him, or distance us from the normal, healthy environment of friendships, projects, and relationships. It simply lets us live in trust, transparency, and compassion.

The experience of God's Spirit as tenderness was mirrored to me quite unobtrusively at a couple's forty-fifth wedding anniversary celebration. The husband and wife had quietly withdrawn sometime during the festivities, and I found them quite by accident. I wasn't looking for them as I passed a sheltered alcove, nor was I eavesdropping—but I was mesmerized by what I saw. There they were, sitting on a loveseat with an overhead light shining indirectly on the man's face. He stared intently at his spouse—that woman about whom he knew everything there was to know: her strengths and weaknesses, her occasional moodiness and temper tantrums, her sense of humor and sense of insecurity, the times she had discreetly refused sexual favors and her moments of erotic lovemaking, her nagging and her magnanimity. Nothing remained hidden.

The expression in the man's eyes conveyed warmth, tenderness, and the same compassion she had shown him during his struggles with John Barleycorn. Not a word was exchanged. She sighed as tears slid down her cheeks. They embraced.

The spirituality of accepted tenderness brings a gathering awareness of the loving gaze of the Abba of Jesus with all the above qualities infinitely magnified, and thus it enables us to be alone with God in the midst of the most diverse activities. It allows an unpretentious presence to the present moment without manuals and mirrors, goals and game plans, stress or distress. *It simply rejoices in the gift.* And this spirituality is all the work of the Spirit defined as "given tenderness."

This tenderness also encompasses an unspoken assurance that Jesus will provide the grace for the next step on the spiritual journey. Charles de Foucauld, a desert hermit and the inspiration for a community known as the Little Brothers of Jesus, wrote, "The one thing we owe absolutely to God is never to be afraid of anything." His unflinching trust in the love of God morphed into humble confidence that the grace for the next step in the dance of life was already there, given. Without anxiety, Abba's children move forward, knowing that the next and the next and the next steps will take care of themselves. Abba's children don't worry about tomorrow or even late this afternoon.

I'm amazed at how long it's taken me to learn this and appalled at how quickly (and how often) I forget it. At the tender age of twenty-one, I was caught up in a romantic relationship with a girl from Brooklyn. I went to Mass every Sunday, braved the sixth commandment (true grit), and settled for a Mexican standoff with an unknown God. If anyone had dared hint that six months later I would be in a Franciscan monastery studying for the priesthood, I would have become catatonic, hidden under the bed, or flagged a taxi to Timbuktu.

During those transitional years, I didn't understand that God's grace always precedes his call. Years later, I looked back and marveled at the relative ease with which Barbara and I had ended the relationship, and the enthusiasm with which I had trundled off to a remote monastery tucked away in the foothills of the Allegheny Mountains. Living in the wisdom of tenderness is an unending adventure in trust and dependence.

The evangelist Robert Frost, speaking at a national conference at Notre Dame, Indiana, chronicled the development of his vocation. In his early twenties, he felt called by God to the ministry. However, because the fear of being sent to Africa as a missionary filled him with dread, he steadfastly resisted the call. Eventually, spiritual exhaustion, ennui, and frustration drove him to the seminary. Several years after ordination, he allowed himself to relax. He was a pastor with tenure. Surely the new breed of young clerics could evangelize Africa quite nicely.

One night he watched a special on television about the Third World. He was captivated. The next day he checked out four books from the public library about Africa and devoured them. If his bishop had called a few weeks later and said, "We'd like you to be an African missionary," he would have replied, "My bags are packed."

What's the message? *God doesn't send you to Africa until he first plants the love of Africa in your heart. Grace always precedes call.*

"Don't be afraid, little flock."

As in a human relationship, tenderness involves a continuing and deepening dependence on God. If the acknowledgment of human contingency is merely theoretical, my illusion of control will endure; if it's operative, I don't have to worry anymore about the means of spiritual growth. All I've to do is expose my frailty, my poverty, and my nothingness to what Chesterton called "the furious love of God." Tenderness is the impeccable sense of feeling safe: it comes from knowing that I'm totally liked and thoroughly loved. If a friend said, "I love you but I don't like you," wouldn't you feel a strong sense of rejection? But God doesn't make such distinctions; he's declared himself unreservedly: "Can a mother forget [reject] her infant, be *without tenderness* for the child of her womb? Even should she forget, I will never forget you" (Isa. 49:15, NAB, italics mine).

Paradoxically, the sense of safety that the acceptance of tenderness engenders is accompanied by a growing loss of control. As we become more comfortable with God's tenderness, we feel the reins on our life loosening and the stranglehold on our autonomous self slipping. The Napoleonic complex (better Saint Helena than second place) no longer roars so ferociously, clamoring for its absurd demands for perfection to be satisfied. There's less need to broadcast our established verities or to impose them on others as absolutes. Our viselike grip on the Yamaha handlebar has relaxed. It's no longer important to endow people we like, possessions we treasure, and institutions we value with superlative qualities; we need not glorify either the past or the future. In the gentle grip of tenderness, we don't invest ourselves in any of those things more than is congruent and appropriate to the way they are. We may even give ourselves a B+ occasionally. That's the sign that self-acceptance is slowly maturing in the wisdom of accepted tenderness.

Furthermore, a subtle but persistent question intrudes on our consciousness: Am I in actuality the primary doer of my own deeds? A significant shift in functional identity slowly stirs within us. We're less the teacher, the computer programmer, the nurse, the physician—and more the celebrant of tenderness. Instead of reacting to persons and things around us, we

respond to the tender Presence that sustains them as it
sustains us.

In his timeless classic *Celebration of Discipline*,
Richard Foster notes, "'Praise the Lord!' is the shout
that reverberates from one end of the Psalter to the
other. Singing, shouting, dancing, rejoicing, adoring—
all are the language of praise." The natural thing to do
when we admire or appreciate something is to praise it.
"What a beautiful sunset!" "Wow! That was a delicious
dinner!" "What a dynamite dancer!" "Isn't Mozart's
music heavenly?" Wonder, awe, delight, admiration,
reverence, appreciation—all these are translated into
praise.

Praise is the festal shout at a lively prayer meeting
developed into a lifestyle. To live in the wisdom of
accepted tenderness is to accept myself and everything
that happens to me as a gift that's good; it's to understand that my very existence is an expression of praise
and thanks to God. Life becomes the divinely written
script of gratitude. "Sing praise to the Lord with all
your hearts. Give thanks to God the Father always and
for everything in the name of our Lord Jesus Christ"
(Eph. 5:19–20). Thanksgiving and praise become a way
of life when we accept God's tenderness. Then it's in

living that we give thanks, and no other thanks are adequate.

Praise as a response to life is beautifully expressed by Francis of Assisi in his luminous "Canticle of Brother Sun":

Most High, omnipotent, good Lord,
To you alone belong praise and glory,
Honor and blessing.
No man is worthy to breathe your name.
Be praised, my Lord, for all your creatures.
In the first place for the blessed Brother Sun,
Who gives us the day and enlightens us through you.
He is beautiful and radiant with his great splendor,
giving witness to you, Most Omnipotent One.
Be praised, my Lord, for Sister Moon and the stars
formed by you so bright, precious and beautiful.
Be praised, my Lord, for Brother Wind
And the airy skies, so cloudy and serene;
for every weather, be praised, for it is life-giving.
Be praised, my Lord, for Sister Water,
So necessary yet so humble, precious and chaste.
Be praised, my Lord, for Brother Fire,
Who lights up the night.

He is beautiful and carefree, robust and fierce.

Be praised, my Lord, for our sister, Mother Earth,

Who nourishes us and watches us

While bringing forth abundance of fruits

with colored flowers and herbs.

Be praised, my Lord, for those who pardon through
    your love

And bear weakness and trial.

Blessed are those who endure in peace,

for they will be crowned by you, Most High.

Be praised, my Lord, for our sister, Bodily Death,

whom no living man can escape.

Woe to those who die in sin.

Blessed are those who discover your holy will.

The second death will do them no harm.

Praise and bless my Lord.

Render thanks.

Serve him with great humility.

Amen.

Paul writes, "Ever since God created the world, his everlasting power and deity—however invisible—have been there for the mind to see in the things he has made" (Rom. 1:20). Like Saint Francis, Paul speaks of the consecration of all of life through Christian praise, and the invasion of the world of the reconciled by the Spirit of Abba, the tenderness of God, flowing from the open heart of the risen Son.

An additional effect of understanding God as the heart of tenderness is reconciliation. Seen from a biblical perspective, reconciliation isn't primarily making up with another person; it's making peace within ourselves in that dimension of our lives where we've previously been unable to find peace.

Reconciliation is the inner healing of our hearts by the tenderness of Jesus. Experientially, it's seldom a sudden catharsis achieved by fingerprinting the forehead; it's not a quick liberation from pain. Neither is it simply learning to be resigned to what we know can never be changed. Rather, it's a gentle growing into a oneness not of our own making. It's a calm joy flowing from an engaged, participatory encounter with the Son of compassion, the only healer in the new Israel of God.

Late one night, when I was directing a spiritual retreat, a seventy-eight-year-old nun knocked on my door. I invited her in and asked, "How may I help you?"

She began to cry. A small, frail woman, she shook with the sobbing. When the tears subsided, she said, "I've never told anyone about this. It started when I was five years old. My father would crawl into my bed with no clothes on. He touched me here and told me to touch him there. [Her pointing fingers left no ambiguity.] He said that our family doctor had suggested touching, so we could know one another better. When I was nine, my father took my virginity, and by the time I was twelve I knew about every kind of sexual perversion that you could find in a dirty book.

"I can't find words to tell you how filthy I feel. I've lived with so much hatred of my father and hatred of myself that I only go to the communion table when my absence there would be conspicuous."

I prayed with her for several minutes for inner healing. Then I asked her, "Sister, would you be willing to go off to a quiet place every morning for the next month, sit down in a chair, close your eyes, upturn your palms, and pray this one phrase over and over: 'Abba, I belong to you'?"

She looked skeptical, so I explained further. "It's a prayer of exactly seven syllables, and seven syllables correspond perfectly to the rhythm of our breathing. Inhale on *Abba;* exhale on *I belong to you.*

"At the outset, you'll say it with your lips alone, but as your mind becomes conscious of the meaning, you'll begin to push your head down into your heart in a figurative sense, so that 'Abba, I belong to you' becomes what the French call *un cri de coeur,* a heartfelt cry from the depth of your being, establishing who you are, why you're here, and where you're going.

"It's a prayer you can pray while working in the garden, listening to music, driving a car, crossing the street, watching television, reading a book, baking a cake, lying in bed. When you pray it dozens and dozens of times each day, and it becomes syncopated with the rhythm of your heartbeat, you can, as Jesus says in Luke 18, pray all day long and never lose heart."

I asked the nun, "Will you try it?"

She replied, "Yes."

Two weeks later, I received the most moving and poetic letter that's ever been written to me. This old woman described the inner healing of her heart, the complete forgiveness of her father, an inner peace she had never known before. She ended her letter this way:

"A year ago, I would have signed this letter with my real name in religious life, Sister Mary Genevieve, but from now on, I'm just Daddy's little girl."

The gentle growing into oneness, the reconciliation with that painful dimension of her past where she couldn't find peace, came about because of the gentle caressing of her memory and the massaging of her heart by the Spirit of Abba poured out from the heart of Jesus Christ. As her example shows us, accepted tenderness prevents us from being tyrants to ourselves, wreaking vengeance on ourselves, enslaving ourselves within the barriers of our fears. Those Christians who have interiorized the tenderness of God become less defensive, more simple and direct, more able to commit themselves, more aware but less afraid of the forces within and around them that drive home their littleness and insignificance.

One of life's greatest paradoxes is that it's in the crucible of pain and suffering that we become tender. Not *all* pain and suffering, certainly. If that were the case, the whole world would be tender, since no one escapes pain and suffering. To these elements must be added mourning, understanding, patience, love, and the willingness to remain vulnerable. Together they lead to wisdom and tenderness.

Instinctively, the heart understands that a healer must have experiential knowledge of the pain that she heals. This instinct is confirmed by Francis MacNutt, a doctor of theology preeminent in the healing ministry. Addressing those involved in the healing ministry of the church, he writes, "Experience indicates that certain people have a special power to pray for certain illnesses but are only fair to middling in praying for other diseases." He cites the case of Michael Gaydos, who, after the healing of his own impaired eyesight, has been effective in healing prayer for those with a similar affliction. "His experience leads us to another interesting conclusion: people who have been healed of a particular ailment seem to have a special gift from that point on in ministering to people with the same problem. Perhaps it is because they now have greater faith in the area in which they themselves have directly experienced God's power."

A further explanation may be that the degree of compassion for the suffering person runs deeper. In praying for chronic alcoholics, I'm frequently overcome by a surge of compassion that I don't ordinarily experience in healing prayer, perhaps because of my own struggle with alcoholism (which has been well documented elsewhere). The damnable imprisonment of not being able to quit, the obsession of the mind and compulsion of the body that paralyze the freedom to choose, the terror of human bondage, the nagging sense of hypocrisy, the guilt, the shame, the loneliness, and the harrowing fear that I've lost God forever are quickly revived when I pray for an alcoholic. Through vicarious suffering a profound rapport is established, and the ineluctable truth, "I am the other," tears down any sense of separation. The healing ministry is a baffling business, and I lay no claim to understanding why some folks get healed and others don't. With my limited experience in this area, I hazard a conjecture: the greater our empathy, the more closely we identify through compassion with the person for whom we pray, the more perfect is our communion with the tender mercy of the healing Christ.

In his definitive work *The Wounded Healer,* Henri Nouwen indicates that grace and healing are communicated through the vulnerability of men and women who have been broken on the wheels of living. The angel in Thornton Wilder's one-act play *The Angel That Troubled the Waters* has a similar message, telling a stricken physician, "Without your wounds, where would your power be? . . . In Love's service only wounded soldiers can serve."

If we follow the instinct that a healer has to know by experience the pain he or she heals, we better understand why there's only one healer in the new Israel of God—Jesus the Lord. Only someone who has known our agony and suffering could by his coming transform that agony into peace. The One who comes to heal has been there and shared every hurt known to humankind.

Intuitively in faith, we grasp the symbol of the tender, redeeming, healing, integrating love of God as embodied in the crucified Savior. "For our sakes God made him who did not know sin to be sin" (2 Cor. 5:21). Every form of sin and its consequences, sickness and disease of every kind, addictions, broken relationships, insecurities, distorted sensuality, hatred, lust, pride, envy, jealousy—all these, on and on, were experienced and carried by "a thing despised and rejected by men" (Isa. 53:3) who knew that nadir of an agony such as no man has ever dreamed. Christ on the cross:

inconceivable what he went through as he hung naked and nailed to the wood.

No one ever died as Jesus did, because he was life itself; no one ever was punished for sin as he was—the sinless one. No one ever experienced the plunge into the vacuum of evil as did Jesus of Nazareth. It will never be given to any human to understand the pain behind the words, "My Father, why have you abandoned me?" or the agony of that death, not simply accepted in patience, but endured screaming to God. And yet "it was our infirmities that he bore, our sufferings that he endured" (Isa. 53:4).

There can never be another healer in the mess and madness of our postmodern world, because no one else has been there. Only Jesus Christ, "a man of sorrows and familiar with suffering," has carried our pain into the peace of grace. He has made peace through the blood of his cross.

But the Father delivered Jesus from sin and death, raised him up and exalted him, "and bestowed on him the name above every other name" (Phil. 2:9). For Jesus, the experience of healing tenderness was an Abba-experience. And so it is with us.

Through the Holy Spirit of given tenderness, we identify with the human Christ and come to know the God of Jesus as our Abba. Every deliverance from darkness and every inner and physical healing should elicit the cry "Abba, Father." We locate the source of the gift of healing tenderness that's come to us, and our faith becomes what French spiritual writer Blaise Arminjon calls "the shuddering certainty of love."

After I shared my thirteen-hour prayer experience with my spiritual director, he closed his eyes and remained silent for several minutes. Then he said, "It's now quite clear in my mind that nothing *really* happens in a person's life until he has experienced and accepted the tenderness of God. Only then can he be tender with God's children."

Recommended Reading

Farrell, Edward. *The Father Is Fond of Me.* Starruga, PA: Dimension Books, 1978.

Foster, Richard. *Celebration of Discipline.* San Francisco: HarperSanFrancisco, 1998.

Keyes, Ken. *Handbook of Higher Consciousness.* Berkeley, CA: Living Love Center, 1972.

Küng, Hans. *On Being a Christian*. New York: Doubleday, 1976.

Nelson, John. *The Little Way of Thérèse of Lisieux*. St. Louis, MO: Liguori Press, 2000.

Tozer, A. W. *The Knowledge of the Holy*. San Francisco: HarperSanFrancisco, 1961.

van Breemen, Peter. *The God Who Won't Let Go*. Notre Dame, IN: Ave Maria Press, 2001.

Chapter Two

THE RING
OF TRUTH

W e're graced and made beautiful by God's irreversible forgiveness, his endless patience, his tender love. We're healed and made whole by the gentle Spirit dwelling within us. We're empowered to live lives of joy and wonder captivated by the undeserved promise of the Kingdom. Everything we have and are as humans and Christians derives from divine goodness and kindness.

What response does the Father seek in return for his relentless tenderness? Personal experience has taught us that illusion and self-deception are no strangers to the spiritual life. What gives the ring of truth and the stamp of authenticity to the Christian's response to Abba's love, the firm assurance that she isn't deceiving herself?

The answer is neither vague nor ambiguous. Speaking first through the voice of his beloved Son, Abba says,

"Come, you have your Father's blessing! Inherit the Kingdom prepared for you from the creation of the world." Why do I declare you blessed and beneficiaries of the Kingdom? Because the only Son I've ever had was hungry and you gave him food, he was thirsty and you gave him a drink. He was a stranger and you welcomed him, naked and you clothed him. He was ill and you comforted him, in prison and you came to visit him. Then you just ones will ask me, "Abba, when did we see your beloved Son hungry and give him food or see him thirsty and give him a drink? When did we welcome him away from home or clothe him in his nakedness? When did we visit him when he was ill or in prison?" I will answer them: "I assure you, as often as you did it for one of your least brothers and sisters, you did it for my only-begotten Son." [Here I've taken the words of Jesus in Matt. 25:34–40 and have them

originate from the Father. The essential meaning of
the passage stays the same.]

To pray Abba in the Spirit is to make our interior
life resemble that of Jesus and to become a son or
daughter in the Son *(filii in Filio)*. "The proof that you
are sons is the fact that God has sent forth into our
heart the spirit of his Son which cries out, 'Abba!'
('Father!')" (Gal. 4:6). With the Spirit in our hearts, we
have a living faith-experience; and living faith, according to Paul, "expresses itself in love" (Gal. 5:6).

Exaggeration and overstatement aren't the dangers
here. Love is the axis of the Christian moral revolution
and the only sign by which the disciple is to be recognized (John 13:35). The danger lurks in our subtle
attempts to minimize, rationalize, or justify our moderation in this regard.

The response the Father seeks to his extravagant
generosity, and the sign that we're living in the wisdom
of tenderness, is that we love, honor, serve, and revere
his only Son as he manifests himself in the least of the
brethren. "The word you hear is not mine; it comes
from the Father who sent me," Jesus tells us (John
14:24). The willingness to live for others is a more

accurate measure of our love for Jesus than ecstasy in prayer. As Thomas Merton put it, "Without love and compassion for others, our own apparent love for Christ is a fiction."

When I live no longer for myself, I can be open to God and open to my neighbor, whom God accepts just as he accepts me.

The question of Who is my neighbor? is dealt with by Jesus in the parable of the good Samaritan (Luke 10:29–37). Interestingly, the conscious awareness of Jesus' presence in the "least of the brethren" is neither expected nor required. The Samaritan assists the mugged man without dragging in religious concerns. He focuses on the man's need without inquiring about the state of his prayer life.

"Lord, when did we see you hungry and feed you?" Those declared blessed at the Last Judgment will have no memory of meeting Jesus in those whom they fed, sheltered, and comforted. They won't remember because in those moments when urgent need surfaced, they forgot themselves. In unselfconscious freedom, they responded to human need without seeking to be noticed, unconcerned about impressing anyone, and unworried about getting gold stars for their behavior. At the Last Judgment, they'll be bewildered to learn that the befuddled old man shuffling around in his shabby apartment, thick-tongued and mumbling about a prescription he needed from the pharmacy, was the Master. It's liberating to learn that we don't have to recognize Jesus in the least brother or sister or bestow some Christ-like quality on the derelict in the doorway. It's also demanding, however. The horizons of Christian concern broaden beyond the morally upright, the potential convert, and the good-natured slob.

The reply to the question Who is my neighbor? plunges us into the scandal of Jesus. The way of tenderness is not chronic niceness, sloppy sentimentality, or a soporific spirituality for the softheaded. The spiritual life isn't a theory. Living the spiritual life, treading the way of tenderness, calls for radical conversion, renunciation of a circumscribed moral code, and a life of humble service.

This isn't a typical picture of the spiritual life, however. In his landmark work, *On Being a Christian*, Hans Küng writes,

The absolutely unpardonable thing was not [Jesus']
concern for the sick, the cripples, the lepers, the
possessed . . . not even his partisanship for the
poor, humble people. The real trouble was that he
got involved with moral failures, with obviously
irreligious and immoral people: people morally and
politically suspect, so many dubious, obscure,
abandoned, hopeless types, on the fringe of every
society. This was the real scandal. Did he really
have to go so far? This attitude in practice is
notably different from the general behavior of religious people.

Clearly, the very foundations of traditional religion
have been shaken. Traitors, swindlers, and adulterers
enter the Kingdom before the religiously respectable.
The depraved prodigal is loved as much as his hard-
working brother, who never frolicked in the fleshpots.
The heretical Samaritan is presented as a model to the
Levitical priesthood. And at the end they all get the
same reward. Righteousness seems to be turned upside
down.

What kind of lunatic justice is this, which abolishes
all sacred standards and reverses all order of rank, mak-

ing the last first and the first last? What kind of naive love is this, which makes no distinction between honorable and dishonorable professions?

Dangerous teaching that reduces the gospel to snippets of truth on a sea of delirium! If the fundamental assumption of Christianity is that God is dotty, then, as e. e. cummings wrote, "Damn everything but the circus!" If the God of Jesus chooses to behave in such a foolish fashion, who can take him seriously? If Jesus forgives so indiscriminately and charges us to do the same, life is a tale told by an idiot and more than anyone can believe. If the Kingdom is accessible to every Tom, Dick, and Harry, then righteousness is bankrupt, human justice is vitiated, and the very roots of religion are upturned.

Such were the protests hurled at Jesus of Nazareth by scores of Palestinian Jews. Flinging accusations of "heretic" and "blasphemer," the cynics, skeptics, and pessimists—sensible folk, all—prevailed. (How blessed are the sensible, then and now: they shall see the very tip of their nose.)

Against all the canons of prudence and discretion, Jesus announced the dawn of a new era, the inbreak of a higher righteousness, the mind-bending manifesto that he had come to call sinners. More alarming still, he claimed that the sinner would be accepted *prior* to any statement of sorrow. First comes grace (given tenderness); then comes the decision to strike out in a new direction.

The fierce mercy of Jesus is at work protecting moral failures from the fierce shaming and moral debasement of religious bureaucrats who have severed spirituality from religion, the heart from the head, and grace from nature. Real sinners deserving real punishment are gratuitously pardoned; they need only accept tenderness already present. Forgiveness has been granted; they need only the wisdom to accept it and repent. These are the ragamuffins, the poor in spirit whom Jesus declared blessed. They know how to accept a gift. "Come, all you who are wiped out, confused, bewildered, lost, beat-up, scarred, scared, threatened, and depressed, and I'll enlighten your mind with wisdom and fill your heart with the tenderness that I have received from my Father." This is unconditional pardon. The sinner need only live confidently in the wisdom of tenderness.

"Grace then comes before law," writes Küng. "Or better, what holds is the law of grace. Only in this way is a new, higher righteousness possible. It begins with unconditional forgiveness: the sole condition is trust inspired by faith or trusting faith; the sole consequence to be drawn is the generous granting of forgiveness to others. Anyone who is permitted to live, being forgiven in great things, should not refuse forgiveness in little things."

The ultimate reason why we must forgive instead of condemn is that God himself does not condemn, but forgives. Because he has freely chosen to put tenderness before law, we're authorized to do the same. In the imagery of the parables, God is presented as the father rushing out to meet his son, the absurdly generous farmer who gives latecomers the same wage as day-long laborers, the judge hearing the prayer of the importunate widow. In the man Jesus, the invisible God becomes visible and audible. And he's seen as a God "whose tender compassion has broken from on high, to shine on those who dwell in darkness and the shadow of death, and to guide our feet on the road to peace" (Luke 1:78–79). The prophet Jesus taught in the power of the Spirit that Christian giving and forgiving should copy God's giving and forgiving. Acceptance is absolute—without inquiry into the past, without special conditions—so that the liberated sinner can live again, accept her self, forgive her self, love her self.

As Christians living in the Spirit, we're called to pass on the tenderness of God. The parameters of our compassion extend beyond those who opt for our lifestyle, favor our existence, or make us feel good. Charges of elitism are dropped for the lack of evidence. Peace and reconciliation for all, without exception— even for moral failures—is the radical lifestyle of Christians living in the wisdom of accepted tenderness. We may be called friends of tax-collectors and sinners—but only because we are (or should be). We understand that we're in the company of some rather honorable people, those sinners; in fact, we're in the company of Jesus himself. According to the gospel, it's unrestrained tenderness and limitless compassion that stamp our relationship with the Father of Jesus as belonging to the order of the Really Real.

That claim has the ring of truth. Like Jesus, it leads us deeper into the Abba-experience.

Chapter Three

CHRIST IN OTHERS

W hat a strange turn of phrase in the thirteenth chapter of John's Gospel: Jesus said, "Love one another as I have loved you" (13:34). Surely it would have been more reasonable to say, "Love me as I have loved you." But he *didn't* say that.

Again in John's first letter we read, "Since God loved us so much, we too should love one another" (4:11). Certainly it would have been more logical for the author to say, "If God loved us so much, so we ought to love him." But he didn't say that either.

Still, what wasn't said would be good, sound human logic, and the logic that we would follow if the New Testament weren't so insistent on its own logic. It runs like this: in the practical order of the Kingdom, the love of God and the love of neighbor are inseparable. "Anyone who says, 'I love God,' and hates his brother is a liar, since a man who does not love the brother that he can see cannot love God, whom he has never seen" (1 John 4:20).

In the winter of 1947, Abbé Pierre, known as the modern apostle of mercy to the poor of Paris, found a young family almost frozen to death on the streets. He scooped them up and brought them back to his own poor dwelling, already crowded with vagrants. Where could he house them? After some thought, he went to the chapel, removed the Blessed Sacrament, and placed it upstairs in a cold, unheated attic. Then he installed the family in the chapel to sleep for the night. When his Dominican confreres expressed shock at such irreverence to the Blessed Sacrament, Abbé Pierre replied, "Jesus Christ isn't cold in the Eucharist, but he is cold in the body of a little child."

We Christians boldly profess that Jesus Christ is present within us, and we cite John 15:4 as a proof text. But Jesus also said that he's present in those around us (Matt. 25:40). Why don't we believe that? We have the same reason for accepting or rejecting both presences—the Word of the Lord Jesus Christ.

The gospel vision is precise on this point: we can't be worshiping some vague deity above the clouds; we can't be acknowledging Jesus Christ living within us and ignoring him in those around us. Two central facts of Christianity emerge—Christ is in you, and Christ is in me—and in the end, as Saint Augustine said, "there will be the one Christ loving himself."

The Lord is in the people with whom we rub shoulders every day, the people whom we think we can read as an open book. Sometimes he's buried there, sometimes he's bound hand and foot there, but he's there. We've been given the gift of faith to detect his presence there, and the Holy Spirit has been poured out into our hearts that we may love him there. For the meaning of our religion is love. Christianity is all about loving, and we either take it or leave it. It's not about worship and morality, except insofar as these things are expressions of the love that causes them both. "It is typical of Jesus," notes Küng, "that love thus becomes the criterion of piety and a person's whole conduct."

Since the so-called Great Commandment combines the love of God and the love of neighbor—"You must love the Lord your God with all your heart, with all

your soul, and with all your mind. This is the greatest
and the first commandment. The second resembles it;
you must love your neighbor as yourself. On these two
commandments hang the whole law, and the Prophets
also" (Matt. 22:35–40)—in an indissoluble unity, it's
impossible to play God and man off against each other.
Before we approach the table of the Lord, Scripture
tells us, we should go and be reconciled first with our
brother or sister and then come and offer our gift (Matt.
5:23–24). God's cause isn't cult, but humankind.

Because of the mysterious substitution of Christ
for the Christian, each encounter with a brother or sister is a real encounter with the risen Lord, an opportunity to respond creatively to the gospel and mature in
the wisdom of tenderness. Time has been given to us to
cause love to grow, and the success of our lives will be
measured by how delicately and sensitively we have
loved. There's no escaping the gospel logic that all our
thoughts, words, and deeds addressed to others are in a
real way addressed to Christ himself.

Isn't it true that each of us lives in a world of our
own—the world of our mind? What a thickly popu-
lated world that can be! And what an unkind one! How
often we're narrow, cold, haughty, unforgiving, and

judgmental. How readily we push Jesus Christ off his judgment seat and take our place there to pronounce on others (though we've neither the knowledge nor the authority to judge anyone).

None of us has ever seen a motive. Therefore, we don't know, we can't do anything more than suspect what inspires the action of another. For this good and valid reason, we're told not to judge. "If you want to avoid judgment, stop passing judgment" (Matt. 7:1). But if we're reckless enough to judge another, we do well to remember the injunction that "your verdict on others will be the verdict passed on you. The measure with which you measure will be used to measure you" (Matt. 7:2–3).

Yet isn't it second nature to judge? Perhaps so. But there's nothing that so resembles truth as falsehood. That's why we so readily believe appearances, gossip, and lies. So though we feel the urge to judge, we aren't equipped to do so fairly.

Don't you suppose that the Virgin Mary was judged? Isn't it likely that the townspeople in Nazareth thought they knew the real nature of the relationship between Joseph and Mary? A fifteen-year-old girl dating an older man, single and pregnant: Wasn't it rather obvious? Did anyone see the mysterious design of God? Did anyone recognize how Mary had consented to bring Jesus Christ into the world by the overshadowing of the Holy Spirit?

There's ample evidence in Luke's Gospel that the penitent woman who washed Jesus' feet in the home of Simon the Pharisee was judged. The men at the table said, "If this man were a prophet, he would know who and what sort of woman this is that touches him—that she is a sinner" (Luke 7:39). Either by hearsay or personal experience, they knew her to be a woman of easy virtue. How the wagging tongues of religious men condemned her! But did anyone see the emptiness in her—an emptiness waiting to be filled with the love of Jesus Christ? The people who judged this penitent woman were judging one of the dearest friends the Lord ever had.

In the Franciscan tradition, the story of Margaret of Cortona parallels that of the penitent woman of Scripture. Margaret would have been a fashionable woman today. For years she lived with a man outside of wedlock, and she had an illegitimate child. The women of Cortona spit on the street when Margaret came to town. But when she encountered the merciful love of the redeeming Lord, she became what I'll never be—a canonized saint, one of the extravagant lovers of God in Christian history.

The point is quite simple: most of the time (because we can't see motives) we're wrong in our judgments about others. The tragedy is that our attention centers on what people are *not*, rather than on what they are and who they might become. As Peter van Breemen notes in *The God Who Won't Let Go*, "We need enormous discipline to let go of our stereotypes, our own advantages, and our expectations to behold the other as she really is." Rash judgment is the enemy of tenderness and compassion; it was vehemently denounced by the Lord Jesus as inimical to the Kingdom lifestyle.

God has invested his children with an extraordinary power through the gift of speech. What power we have with our words to bless or to curse, to affirm or to reject, to revere or to blaspheme God!

The oft-told story of Zacharias Werner, which I encountered in Dorothy Gies McGuigan's *Metternich and the Duchess*, offers a vivid illustration of the awesome power of the spoken word. A romantic poet turned priest, Werner packed Vienna's churches in

1809 with his fiery sermons on carnal sin. One Sunday he preached to a huge congregation a sermon on "that tiny piece of flesh, the most dangerous appurtenance of a man's body." Gentlemen blanched, ladies blushed, as he elaborated on the horrendous consequences of its misuse, his piercing eyes shooting sparks as he expounded graphically, on and on.

Toward the end of his sermon, Werner leaned over the pulpit to scream at his listeners, "Shall I name you that tiny piece of flesh?" There was paralyzed silence. Smelling salts were extracted from ladies' handbags. He leaned out farther, and his voice rose to a hoarse shout: "Shall I show you that tiny piece of flesh?" Horrified silence! Not a whisper or a rustle of a prayer book could be heard. Werner's voice dropped, and a smile slid over his face. "Ladies and gentlemen, behold the source of our sins!" And he stuck out his tongue.*

Perhaps Jesus, dwelling in the least of the brethren, is slashed by our words more painfully than he was by the Roman soldiers at Golgotha. How we cause him to

---

* McGuigan, Dorothy Gies. *Metternich and the Duchess.* New York: Doubleday, 1966.

squirm under the things we say, using him as the butt of our jokes and doing harm, by our words and actions, to those he loves.

When Jesus said that he was hungry and thirsty and naked in those around us, he was referring to more than mere corporal needs. We're surrounded by people who are hungry and thirsty and naked in their souls, and they come to us hungry for understanding, thirsty for affirmation, naked with loneliness, and wanting to be covered with the mantle of our genuine tenderness. I shudder at the times, too numerous to count, that I've refused to give such aid to them. Entranced in self-absorption, I've often been unavailable to their hopes, fears, dreams, joys, aspirations, and disappointments.

As the years pass by, I find myself growing more impatient and moving at a more hurried pace. The imposter, the sinister impersonator of my true self, has reappeared in the guise of a self-important persona who has an urgent mission to accomplish and an empire to build. Others may have idle time to entertain small talk and chitchat. I, however, am quarterbacking the A-team with the sole agenda of getting into the end zone as expeditiously as possible. Intolerance of the blunders of others isn't only just but salutary. "Why?" you may ask. Because the incompetence of others reflects on my credibility!

Although he has no ontological reality, the imposter often succeeds in making a nest in my consciousness. He's smitten with his honorary doctorate; he personifies the admiration of people who think well of me; he's the sum of all the ministerial successes that give me identity. When I present this false self in prayer, God doesn't bless what doesn't exist. If I summon the courage to be still, my true self whispers, "All that matters today is patience, kindness, tenderness, and compassion."

Dietrich Bonhoeffer, writing in *Life Together* about community life during the Nazi years, didn't mince words:

Nobody is too good for the meanest service. One who worries about the loss of time that such petty, outward acts of helpfulness entail is usually taking the importance of his own career too solemnly. We must be ready to allow ourselves to be interrupted by God. . . . It is a strange fact that Christians and even ministers frequently consider their work so important and urgent that they will allow nothing to disturb them. They think they are doing God a service in this, but actually they are disdaining God's "crooked but straight path" (Gottfried Arnold). It is part of the discipline of humility that we must not spare our hand where it can perform a service and that we do not assume that our schedule is our own to manage, but allow it to be arranged by God.

Humility and fraternal love are spiritual bedfellows. When we befriend our own brokenness and minister to our wounds with tenderness and compassion, the "other" is no longer an intruder but a fellow sufferer.

It's virtually impossible to miss the intensity in Jesus' voice when he says, "It is not those who say to me, 'Lord, Lord' who will enter the kingdom of heaven, but the person who does the will of my Father in heaven" (Matt. 7:21). Since we have little evidence that Jesus spent a lot of time in church and abundant evidence that he went about doing good, and since compassion is not about feeling sorry for people or nodding "Yes, yes" behind the daily paper while someone stands in front of us trying to have their heart "heard" (to use

Benedictine nun and author Joan Chittister's example), it seems safe to say that the will of the Father is to spend each day loving in deed, as Jesus did.

Do I spend my days loving? I put this hard question to myself during a recent sojourn in solitude. Traveling all over the country preaching the gospel and writing books on the spiritual life is a high-profile ministry rife with inherent risks. There's affirmation in a measure of recognition, a burst of applause. And, yet, as I faced this issue during my retreat, I had to ask myself—or, as my Irish relations would say, *himself*— Does the rhetoric I employ to describe life in the Spirit match the reality of my daily discipleship? Have I grown complacent with what I give because it conceals what I withhold? Have I snookered myself into thinking that writing about tenderness automatically transforms my costive heart? Truth to tell, *do I spend my days loving?*

After some soul-searching and a candid session with my spiritual director, I concluded that the answer is yes. Daily I *do* go about loving.

However, there exists a problem of epic biblical proportions: I've divided the human community into certain categories. There are a few people whom I love, a number whom I like, and a multitude whom I seldom think about, move proactively toward, or manifest any concern for. Yet the evangelical witness described in Matthew and Luke quashes discrimination of any kind. "If all you do is love the lovable, do you expect a bonus?" Jesus asks. "Anybody can do that. If you simply say hello to those who greet you, do you expect a medal? Any run-of-the-mill sinner can do that" (Matt. 5:46–47, *The Message*). Any of us can love someone with whom we have a mutual interest or attraction. I find it effortless to turn on to people who favor my existence and make me feel good. So did the contemptible tax-collectors, traitors to the Jewish cause.

One Christmas Eve I was working with a rescue team in the Bowery of New York City, fishing drunks out of the street. In a grimy doorway the stench of one particular alcoholic was so vile that I asked my partner, an agnostic social worker, if he would handle that one. "No trouble," he answered. Whispering tender words of consolation, he gently lifted the drunk into the van. I decided to wait awhile before telling my partner about the power of the Holy Spirit in my life, about seeing Christ in the least and lowliest.

We're not speaking to a minor matter here. Love of others lies at the heart of the Christian moral revolution. The litmus test of our love for God is our love of neighbor. In *The Divine Conspiracy*, a book that Richard Foster said he had been searching for all his life, Dallas Willard writes, "The positive characterization of the kingdom attitude is agape love. . . . Jesus calls us to him to impart himself to us. He does not call us to do what he did, but to be who he was, permeated with love. Then the doing of what he said and did becomes the natural expression of who we are in him."

During his last discourse in the Book of Glory, Jesus says, "I give you a new command: Love one another. In the same way I loved you, you love one another. This is how everyone will recognize that you are my disciples—when they see the love you have for each other" (John 13:34–35, *The Message*).

The truest test of our faith is the way we are with each other every day. When the primacy of love is subordinated to doctrinal correctness and orthodox exegesis, cool cordiality and polite indifference masquerade as love among theologians, biblical scholars, and faculties across the land. When absolute control and rigid obedience pose as love within the family and the local faith-community, we produce trained cowards rather than Christian persons.

During World War II, an American Marine, badly wounded on the island of Saipan, lay bleeding to death. A Navy corpsman rushed to his aid. At the risk of his own life, the corpsman played the good Samaritan, pouring oil and wine on the wounds of his bleeding brother.

It would be an understatement to report that the Marine was neither grateful nor gracious. He demanded to know what had taken the corpsman so damn long to get to him. When the battle subsided, the regimental commander, who had watched the scene from the safety of a bunker, approached the corpsman and said, "Kid, I wouldn't have done that for a million dollars!"

The corpsman's glorious answer: "Neither would I."

He had learned his lesson well. Maybe he didn't know that what he was doing for the unknown soldier, he was doing for Jesus Christ. What matters is that he *acted*. The deed was done. "My brothers, what good is it to profess faith without practicing it?" asks James. "Such faith has no power to save one, has it? If a brother or sister has nothing to wear or no food for the day, and you say to them, 'Goodbye and good luck! Keep warm and

well fed,' but do not meet their bodily needs, what good
is that? So it is with the faith that does nothing in practice. It is thoroughly lifeless" (James 2:14–17).

If we're as serious as was Francis of Assisi about
growing in the wisdom of tenderness, we might do well
to take his peace prayer off the wall and hang it in our
heart, make it the wisdom by which we live:

Lord, make me an instrument of your peace.
Where there is injury, let me bring pardon;
where there is hatred, love,
where there is doubt, faith,
where there is despair, hope,
where there is darkness, light,
where there is sadness, joy.
O Divine Master, grant that I may not seek so much
*   to be consoled as to console,*
to be understood as to understand,
to be loved as to love;
for it is in giving that we receive,
it is in pardoning that we are pardoned,
and it is in dying that we are born to eternal life.

Recommended Reading

Bonhoeffer, Dietrich. *Life Together.* New York: Harper & Row, 1954.

McGuigan, Dorothy Gies. *Metternich and the Duchess.* New York: Doubleday, 1966.

Willard, Dallas. *The Divine Conspiracy.* San Francisco: HarperSanFrancisco, 1998.

Chapter Four

THE IMPOSSIBLE DREAM

When theologians speak of the Trinity, they typically attribute the work of creation to the Father, the work of redemption to the Son, and the work of sanctification—that is, the work of forming Christ within us—to the Holy Spirit.

The Father's creative role as the source of life, the author of all that is, is emphasized in liturgical prayer with invocations such as "Father, you are holy indeed, the fountain of all holiness" and "Abba, you are the fullness of compassion, and all creation rightly gives you praise. All life and holiness come from you through your Son, Jesus Christ." Both the Apostles' Creed and the Nicene Creed begin with a reference to the Father's creative power. In the latter, worshipers say, "We believe in one God, the Father, the Almighty, maker of heaven and earth, of all that is, seen and unseen. . . ." There's no need to multiply examples of what is patently an integral part of our Christian faith: the Abba of Jesus is the Creator of the universe and the source of all life and holiness in the world.

The source of all life: every time we see a tiny plant burgeoning in springtime or witness the miracle of a newborn baby, we see the loving hand of the Father at work. It's relatively easy for the faith-filled Christian to recognize the presence and activity of the heavenly Father when physical and visible life is the issue. It's more subtle but no less real when spiritual, invisible, unseen life is the subject. Let's turn our attention to a dramatic and powerful example of the life-creating activity of the Father in the unseen world of the human spirit.

When I first saw the play *The Man of La Mancha*, based on Miguel Cervantes' *Don Quixote de la Mancha*, I was blown away. In this beautiful story, Don Quixote befriends Aldonza—a street urchin, a trollop, a girl filled with shame and disgust because of her promiscuous past. Having lost every trace of dignity and every vestige of self-respect, Aldonza is consumed with shame and remorse. Don Quixote strides into her life and, for utterly unselfish reasons, attempts to befriend her and to awaken in her a sense of dignity, worth, and purpose. But all his efforts are in vain. She rebuffs him at every turn.

Don Quixote coins an endearing nickname for Aldonza, calling her his "Dulcinea"—his sweet little one. Other times he calls her "my lady," to give her a sense of aristocratic bearing. One day he calls out both names with a flourish.

When Aldonza hears him, she storms into the room and tells him, in no uncertain terms, exactly how *un*ladylike she is. As she describes a past that includes a mother who abandoned her, a father whose identity is unknown, and men who paid her for their brief acquaintance, she reveals just how little she thinks of herself.

She then chides Don Quixote for his efforts to better her. What good are dreams, after all, to someone with no hope of achieving them? She sees herself as unworthy of being anything but the nobody she is.

But that's not how the Father sees this wounded, frightened creature—his own creation—and it's not how he wants her to see herself. It's the Father's vital, creative, life-giving power in Don Quixote, mediated to him through Jesus Christ by the working of the Holy Spirit, that revives Aldonza, restores her sense of personal dignity, and resurrects her to newness of life.

But in one of life's tragic ironies, Don Quixote falls desperately ill—his mind weary from having thought too much, his body wounded from having fought too much, his heart broken from having loved too much.

Aldonza hurries to his bedside to offer comfort. (Did she remember the words of Jesus in the Upper Room? "If anyone loves me, she will keep my word, and my Father will love her, and we shall come to her and make our home with her"—John 14:23.) Abba/ Creator, dwelling within the graced soul of Aldonza (and thereby making her Dulcinea indeed) is with her, helping her to breathe new life into Don Quixote.

She kneels down and pleads with Don Quixote to remember his dream for her, his dream for Dulcinea. Hoping that if she can rekindle that dream in him, its heat will bring him back to life, she reminds him repeatedly of the grace and glory that he saw in her, that he tried to call out from her.

Don Quixote stirs, remembering. Then, taking in her words and her manner, he dares to hope that what he envisioned for her might have been more than a dream.

Aldonza prompts him further, reminding him of the quest he often spoke of—a quest of bravery and honor and adventure. Finally the dream catches fire in Don Quixote again and he speaks once more of his glorious quest. Stronger now, and ready for further adventure, he calls to his faithful squire, Sancho, and requests his sword and armor. Then he rises, reborn.

The creative power of the Father's love dwelling in Aldonza through the Spirit of Jesus Christ has rekindled the dying flame in the heart of the Man of La Mancha, and he resumes his quest. To his death he will pursue his impossible dream.

In John's Gospel Jesus says, "I am the way, and the truth, and the life. No one comes to the Father but through me" (John 14:6). Jesus is the way to the Father; he is the truth of the Father, for as he said, "I do not speak my own truth but the word of the One who sent me" (John 14:24). Jesus is the life of the Father because all life and all holiness come from

Abba's creative hand. Jesus came to share that life with us. "I came that they may have life and have it to the full" (John 10:10).

Jesus lived and died and rose in order that we might be filled with the Spirit of life—his own life— the life of his Abba. Paul writes in First Corinthians, "Scripture has it that Adam the first man became a living soul; the last Adam has become a life-giving Spirit" (15:45). The Spirit is life itself. When Paul writes in First Thessalonians, "Do not stifle the Spirit" (5:19), he is saying, "Do not stifle life." Reverence for life is synonymous with reverence for the Father, the source of life. Human life is incomparably sacred because it mirrors divine life as no other life can.

The gift of life is a sharing in him who is Life, in the God whose God-ness is summed up in the phrase "He who is." We live because he lives. Thus, all of God's creation cries out, "Handle me with reverence." For this reason Christians living in the wisdom of tenderness are especially sensitive to life at its dawning and life in its twilight, in the rights of the unborn and the dignity of the age-worn. Because they're sensitive to the life-giving Spirit (the tenderness of God), because they revere the Abba of Jesus, they're filled with sensitivity and reverence for *all* life. I submit that this vision is basic to a proper definition of the Spirit-filled Christian.

Given this definition, what are we to make of the pro-life, pro–death penalty conundrum? What are we to think when, for example, life imprisonment without parole is offered as an alternative to lethal injection, and the latter is preferred by Christians who take a pro-life stance when it comes to the unborn? Clearly, all too often the Christian community's pro-life posture is selective, inconsistent, and vulnerable to unbiased criticism. Ethicist Richard B. Hays writes, "One reason the world finds the New Testament of peacemaking and love of enemies incredible is that the church is so massively faithless. On the question of violence, the church is deeply compromised and committed to nationalism, violence, and idolatry." Citing Paul's letter to the Romans, Hays comments, "Those who are members of the one body in Christ (12:5) are never to take vengeance (12:19). . . . There is not a syllable in the Pauline letters that can be cited in support of Christians employing violence."

The anti-abortion stance of the Christian community flows from a Spirit-filled reverence for the Father of

Jesus. No man or woman may arrogate to him/herself the right to determine the duration of life of an unborn child or an age-worn parent. The decision to reclaim the gift of life lies within the sovereign dominion of the Father. However, it's naive and overly simplistic to equate a Spirit-filled reverence for life with an anti-abortion stance. Opposition to abortion is certainly an integral aspect of reverence for life, but the two terms are neither synonymous nor co-extensive. What makes the pro-life position of so many believing Christians unbelievable in the eyes of millions is that it's so frighteningly selective. When we say that we hold life sacred, that we reverence life, that we're pro-life, that we're for the Father, the world at large questions our credibility. Why? Because our Christian conscience isn't *catholic,* in the pristine sense of being appropriately universal. Embryonic life, fetal life, ah yes: handle with care, don't touch, and defend with every weapon in the Christian arsenal! Other life? Well, that depends.

There are three areas where our reverence for life is less than compelling. The Christian equivalent of Watergate, these areas deface our image as sons and daughters of the Father and give the lie to our pro-life protestations. And it's in precisely these three areas that the spirituality of tenderness calls the Christian to undiscriminating witness in the pro-life debate.

The first area is that of Jewish life. Here we must be both honest and sensitive. The Jewish community today still remembers that in the first three centuries of our Christian era, there was a widespread conviction that the Jews had killed Christ, and that because the Jews had rejected the Messiah they were themselves rejected by God, a people accursed. The Jewish people remember the tradition of Christian hostility and contempt that was expressed in the homilies of one of the church's most remarkable preachers and saints, John Chrysostom. In the year A.D. 387, he thundered from a pulpit in Antioch,

> I know that a great number of the faithful have for the Jews a certain respect and hold their ceremonies in reverence. This provokes me to eradicate completely such a disastrous opinion. I have already brought forward that the synagogue is worth no more than a theater; . . . it is a place of prostitution. It is a den of thieves and a hiding

place of wild animals, . . . not simply of animals but of impure beasts. . . . God has abandoned them. What hope of salvation have they left?

They say that they too worship God but this is not so. None of the Jews, not one of them, is a worshipper of God. . . . Since they have disowned the Father, crucified the Son, and rejected the Spirit's help, who would dare to assert that the synagogue is not the home of demons? God is not worshipped there. It is simply a house of idolatry. The Jews live for their bellies, they crave for the goods of this world. In shamelessness and greed they surpass even pigs and goats. . . . The Jews are possessed by demons, they are handed over to impure spirits. . . . Instead of greeting them and addressing them as much as a word, you should turn away from them as from a pest and a plague of the human race.

The sensitive Jew remembers the Middle Ages: every Jewish ghetto ever structured by Christians, every forced baptism, every Crusade to liberate the Holy Places, every Good Friday pogrom, every forced exodus (such as that of 1492), every portrait of Shylock exacting his pound of flesh, every accusation of deicide, every identifying dress or hat or badge, every death for conscience' sake, every back turned or shoulder shrugged, every sneer or slap or curse. And the sensitive Jew remembers what the brilliant scholar Rabbi Marc Tannenbaum has phrased so forcefully:

> One must confront ultimately how a country, when it vaunted its great values and its great moral traditions, spoke of itself as a country of ancient Christian culture, which was in fact the seat of the Holy Roman Empire for almost a millennium, beginning with Charlemagne—it was possible for millions of Christians to sit by as spectators while millions of human beings who were their brothers and sisters, the sons of Abraham according to the flesh, were carried out to their death in the most brutal, inhuman, uncivilized ways. And one must confront as one of the terrible facts of the history of this period the conversation that took place between Adolph Hitler and two bishops in April, 1933, when they began raising questions about the

German policy toward the Jews and Hitler said to them, as reported in the book *Hitler's Table Talk*, that he was simply completing what Christian teaching and preaching had been saying about the Jews for the better part of 1,900 years. "You should turn away from them as from a pest and a plague of the human race," said St. John Chrysostom, and 1,500 years later thousands of his disciples implemented his teaching literally.

With this tragic history as background, are you surprised that countless Jews are unimpressed by our anti-abortion stance, by our arguments for the sanctity and sacredness of human life? Can you blame them for suggesting a certain hypocrisy—all the more discouraging because it's still unrecognized, unfelt? Is anyone listening? Does anyone care? Jews are indeed listening, but they hear more than our contemporary rhetoric. They hear cries of "Christ-killer," they feel lashes on their back, they see human soap, they taste hunger, they smell gas. Jews do care—their whole history is a story of caring—but they're not at all sure that *we* care, or that we care for them.

What to do? There's no simple answer here. Theologian Walter Burghardt,* described once as "the grand old man of American homiletics," has suggested that the Christian community needs a fresh theology of Judaism and its destiny; we need a profound sense of sorrow for our un-Christian past; we need far more contact, more dialogue with Jews than we've yet achieved; we need to understand that anti-Semitism is Christian spit on the face of our Jewish Savior; but perhaps, above all, we need to live out what William Shakespeare phrased so realistically in *The Merchant of Venice:*

Hath not a Jew eyes? Hath not a Jew hands, organs, dimensions, senses, affections, passions? Is not a Jew fed with the same food, hurt with the same weapons, subject to the same diseases, healed by the same means, warmed and cooled by the same winter and summer, as a Christian is? If you prick

* In this section on Jewish life, enemy life, and the quality of life, I'm quoting Burghardt verbatim, or almost verbatim. I've read through six of his books and can't find the source. Otherwise, I would gratefully acknowledge that this wonderful man actually wrote most of the words in this section. Please forgive me, Walter. I have no intention of plagiarizing.

him, does he not bleed? If you tickle him, does he not laugh? If you poison him, does he not die?

The second area in which our Christian reverence for life is less than compelling is in our dealings with "the enemy." Here again history calls us to an account that we haven't faced with sufficient candor. I don't intend to beat a dead horse by resurrecting the issue of the morality of the war in Vietnam or of the U.S. involvement in Cambodia. I'm concerned rather with the strange image we've projected in the past forty years—an anti-life image. Not *all* Christians, of course. Such a charge would be slander. After all, we heard the impassioned cry at the United Nations: "No more war! War never again!" Christians across the world have condemned the senseless slaughter of innocents. And the Christian population as a whole has lifted its arms unceasingly to heaven in passionate prayer for peace. Yet despite our prayers for peace, we've done precious little to achieve it.

Oh sure, we've long been convinced that war is hell. We've long felt that there's something tragically wrong when the governments of the world spend hundreds of billions of dollars a year to kill the life given by the Father, to threaten, to deter, to keep peace; when Palestinian Muslims dance for joy in the streets following a devastating terrorist attack; when innocent American followers of Islam are savagely beaten by crazed citizens seeking retribution; when three million refugees water the roads and rice paddies with their tears; when human beings are tortured by other human beings. We weep when we learn that one out of five American children goes to bed hungry.

Where, then, have we failed? Simply in limiting our compassion. Compassion is a gift we offer our *friends*. The wisdom of tenderness is dismissed as inappropriate or irrelevant when the enemy is at the gate. When the war drums rattle, Abba's child feels compelled to abandon childhood, forsake any sense of radical dependence on divine providence, and take control. He's convinced that nothing good is going to happen unless he himself makes it happen. As poet and peace activist Daniel Berrigan notes,

> We grow out of childhood into war. We grow out of the God of childhood into homage toward the gods of war. The gods of our adulthood are diplomatic, which is to say glib, mendacious, insipid,

tedious, mealy-mouthed. Or they are bellicose—
truculent, cocksure, grisly, treacherous, callous,
ferocious. One kind or another, such gods drive us
toward moral oblivion.

In this ethical disarray, the role of Christianity is
seen as merely blessing and encouraging the national
will. The moral numbing brought on by adjusting to
the world and its devious language of "measured response and sensible action" can barely be perceived in
the din of tumultuous patriotism. During the Korean
War, my training in the Marine Corps was devoted to
achieving glory by killing "gooks"—and neither the
task nor the label was repugnant to me or my fellow
jarheads.

One morning not so long ago, I experienced a
bad—a *very* bad—hour. I asked myself how often
between 1950 and 1999 I had wept over a North
Korean or a North Vietnamese, over a neo-Nazi skin-
head or a religious fanatic in a fortified compound. I
couldn't remember a single instance. It was then that I
wept—not for them, but for me.

When we laud life, when we blast abortion, is anyone listening, does anyone care? Not among those

people on whom our power rests more heavily than our compassion, not in Nagasaki or Hiroshima. To them we're a contradiction. On the one hand, we proclaim the love and the anguish, the pain and the joy that go into fashioning a single child; we proclaim how precious each life is to God and should be to us. On the other hand, when it's enemy soldiers who shriek to Allah with their flesh in flames, we neither weep nor are ashamed; instead, we call for more.

The third area in which we Christians fail is in our efforts to improve the quality of life. Here again our gospel, our Good News, falls on deaf ears because the Christian image is poor. Increasingly over the past five years, as discussions on abortion have degenerated into hate-filled conflicts with no holds barred, my non-Christian friends—especially those who work with the poor, the crippled, and the addicts—have thrown into my face the selfsame theme:

You Christians keep mouthing the immorality of abortion, but how many of you are involved in the consequences of your moral absolutes? The thirteen-year-old girl raped in the alley, the teen-agers utterly unprepared to raise children, the

millions of unwanted children, the children beaten
with belts and roasted on stoves, the children
whose bellies are forever bloated with hunger. You
prattle about reshuffling the world's resources,
while India grows by thirteen million a year and
139 of its infants die for every thousand births. Are
you listening? Do you care?

If you do, why do so many of you keep moving
away from the problem, out of the city and into the
suburbs, out of the public schools and into the
private, out of the arena where your morality is
so productive? For many of us, tenderness has
become a cliché and mercy an abstraction. To quote
one of our heroes, Mohandas Gandhi, "We like
your Christ but not your Christians, because they're
so unlike your Christ."

Obviously such rhetoric obscures the fact that the
church is intimately involved in all these issues. We
don't insist that a child be born humanely and then
willingly permit her to grow up or die inhumanely. The
pluriform witness of American Christians in the inner
city, the unsung dedication to the mentally and physically impaired, the help offered to unwed mothers and

illegitimate children, the unparalleled compassion shown to the widows and children of New York City's firefighters and police officers—all these, and innumerable other compassionate gestures, reveal the Christian heart. And yet our impressive track record highlights a tragic fact difficult to deny: we Christians have not given to the quality of life nearly the same attention, the priority, that we've given to sheer, naked life itself.

That deficiency, I'm convinced, is explained by the limits that we've placed on our love and our reverence for life. Our love for human beings, Jesus told us, will be the sacrament, the visible sign that he's among us. This is how the world will recognize him. And the world *doesn't* see him because the world doesn't see our love. Whole cities could live on the garbage from our dumps, on the clothes we wear once and then discard, on the luxuries that we've made necessities. Blacks and whites exist in uneasy truce because we Christians have been as color-conscious as our unbelieving neighbors. For so many of us a court of law is more effective than the Sermon on the Mount. There's no evidence that we Christians eat less, drink less, lust less, hate less than the men and women who are uncommitted to Jesus and his radical way of life.

And we shout more stridently when an abortion bill comes before the legislature than when, as happened one weekend in Arkansas, a black family was shotgunned out of a white neighborhood.

Here again our prayer meetings are compromised by the broader Christian context. The inescapable emphasis, the thrilling stress on life in the Spirit that's so believable within our meetings, becomes less credible the minute we step outside. I'm not ready to demand a new priority: no life unless quality can be guaranteed in advance. But I do ask, and I believe that the Spirit of Jesus asks likewise, for a fresh commitment to quality of life. We must indeed continue to raise our voices in protest against what we see as the unjustified destruction of the unborn; but if the protest of the believing Christian stops there, if that's the sum and substance of our reverence for the Father and his gift of life, then our conscience must forever worry away at us.

Two impractical but powerful suggestions: First, reflect ever more frequently on how near to God is the life of suffering man—so near that Rabbi Abraham Heschel could say shortly before his death, "There is an old idea in Judaism that God suffers when man suffers. There is a famous text saying that even when a criminal

is hanged on the gallows, God cries. God identifies himself with the misery of man." The Father cares for the life he has created. We can help God by reducing human suffering, human anguish, and human misery.

Allow me to share briefly the story of a man who not only reduced my sufferings but saved my life. I call him my Man of La Mancha.

In April 1975, I lay desperately sick on a condominium floor in Fort Lauderdale, Florida. Later, I learned that within a few hours, if left unattended, I would have gone into alcoholic convulsions and might have died. Incredible as it sounds, until that point in time I hadn't realized that I was an alcoholic. I had assumed that all alcoholics were street bums, mumbling incoherently to themselves and clutching a bottle of cheap wine wrapped in a paper bag. (Only later did I learn that such folks constitute a mere three percent of active alcoholics.)

I crawled to the telephone but was shaking so violently that I couldn't dial the numbers on the rotary phone. Finally I managed one digit and got the operator. "Please help me," I pleaded. "Call Alcoholics Anonymous." She took my name and address and promised to do as I asked.

Within twenty minutes a man walked in the door. I had never seen him before, and he had no idea who I was. But he had the breath of the Father on his face and an immense reverence for my life. He scooped me up in his arms and raced me to the detox center of a local hospital. There began the long days of medically supervised withdrawal. The chronic alcoholic who tries to quit cold turkey is highly susceptible to a heart attack or stroke. Anyone who has been down both sides of the street will tell you that unsupervised withdrawal from alcohol is no less severe than unsupervised withdrawal from heroin.

I'll spare the reader the details of that odyssey of shame and pain, of unbearable guilt, remorse, and humiliation. But that stranger brought me back to life. His words might sound corny to the uninitiated, but they were words of life to me. This fallen-away Christian, who hadn't been to church in many, many years, told me that the Father loved me, that he hadn't abandoned me, that he would draw good from what had happened. He told me that the name of the game right then wasn't guilt, fear, and shame but survival. He told me to forget about what I had lost and focus on what I had left.

He gave me an article from the June 1957 *Journal of the American Medical Association* which explained that alcoholism is a bio/psychological disease and that alcoholics are biologically different from other people. Once alcoholics take the first drink, the phenomenon of craving develops and they become impotent to stop. That caring stranger told me to feel no more guilt than if I were recovering from some other disease, such as cancer or diabetes. Above all else, he affirmed me in my emptiness, loved me in my loneliness, and taught me—a broken-down drunk—the wisdom of tenderness.

Again and again he told me of the Father's love—how when his children stumble and fall, he doesn't scold them but scoops them up and comforts them. Later I learned that my benefactor was an itinerant laborer who mowed lawns for a living. Barely able to scrape by, he put cardboard in his work shoes to cover the holes. Yet, when I was able to eat again, he bought me my first dinner at McDonald's. For five days and five nights, he breathed life into me physically and spiritually and asked nothing in return.

This man who gave me so much had lost his family and fortune through drinking. Years after he'd worked his way back from the bottom, he was still alone and lonely, as his evening routine attests: He would turn on his TV for company, talking to John Wayne in hopes that he'd talk back. Before bed he would spend fifteen minutes reading a meditation book, then praise God for his mercy, thank him for what he had left, and pray for all alcoholics. As his final act of the day, he would go to his window, raise the shade, and bless the world.

Two years later, after treatment in the Hazelden, Minnesota, Alcohol and Drug Rehabilitation Center, I went down to Clearwater Beach, Florida, to work on my second book, *The Gentle Revolutionaries*. Some friends had offered me a townhouse on a remote part of the beach, where I could be alone to craft the words. Back in his neck of the woods, I tried to get in touch with my Man of La Mancha.

Through the AA grapevine I learned that this life-saving friend, whom I'll call Mephisto, had moved from southern to central Florida, but I had no address or telephone number for him. I called the central office of AA in Clearwater and was able to track him down. I learned that, in one of life's sad ironies, Mephisto was twenty-seven miles away on Skid Row in Tampa. The voice at the central office explained that Mephisto had been twelve-stepping too often—a term based on the twelfth step of the AA program, which involves bringing the message of recovery to practicing alcoholics; in other words, Mephisto had been caring for others so much that he forgot to care for himself. There's a buzzword within the AA fellowship: HALT. It's a reminder not to let yourself get too hungry, angry, lonely, or tired, or you'll be especially vulnerable to that first drink. My friend had gotten burned out from helping others and had gone back on the sauce.

I drove to Tampa and parked in the seedy area I hoped to find Mephisto in. As I walked along Skid Row, I spotted a man diagonally across the street who looked like Mephisto—same build, same white hair, about ten years older than I. I headed through traffic to greet him. It wasn't Mephisto, though; I could see that as I approached. Just another wino—neither sober nor drunk, just dry. He hadn't had a drink in twenty-four hours, and his hands twitched and trembled (symptoms that, from personal experience, I call the tinglies and the crawlies). He grabbed my arm and begged, "Hey, man, can you gimme a dollar? I gotta get some wine."

I knelt before him and took his hands in mine. I looked into his eyes, which filled with tears at the unexpected civil human contact. Then I leaned forward and kissed his hands, and he began to cry. He didn't really want wine; he wanted what I'd wanted two years earlier, lying on the condominium floor—to be accepted in his brokenness, to be affirmed in his worthlessness, to be loved in his loneliness. He wanted to be relieved of what Mother Teresa of Calcutta, with her vast personal experience of human misery, said is the worst suffering of all—the feeling of not being accepted or wanted. I never found Mephisto that day, but I was the instrument God used to get that wino into detox.

Two weeks later, I was hosting a meeting in my temporary home for a group of recovering alcoholics on the eleventh step, which reads, "Sought through prayer and meditation to improve our conscious contact with God as we understood him, praying only for knowledge of his will for us and the power to carry that out." Once we discovered that the six of us were all either Episcopalians or Catholics, we decided to celebrate Eucharist. Midway through the service, Mephisto walked up the stairs of the townhouse. You know how your heart skips when you see someone you really care for? My heart went skippity-hop, skippity-hop. He motioned for us not to stop but to continue the worship, so with a smile of welcome we did. A few minutes later, with my back turned to him during the Eucharist, I heard the downstairs door quietly close, and Mephisto was gone. My heart sank.

The next morning I found a letter from him, slipped under the front door. It read, in part,

Last night, in my clumsy way, I came to your house and just prayed for the right to belong among you good people. . . . You will never know what you did for me two weeks ago in Tampa. You didn't see me, but I saw you. I was standing twenty yards away and hiding behind a lamppost.

Brennan, when I saw you kneel down and kiss that wino's hands, you wiped away from my eyes the blank stare of the breathing dead. When I saw that you really cared, my heart began to grow wings—small wings, feeble wings, but wings. I had a pint of Gallo wine in my hand, and I tossed it in a trash bin. You breathed life into me, and I want you to know that. You released me from my shadow world of panic, fear, and self-hatred.

If you should ever wonder who Mephisto is, remember that I am someone you know very well: I am every man you meet and every woman you meet. . . . Am I also you?

Then he ended his letter with a phrase he had never used before in our friendship, "Wherever I go, sober by the grace of God one day at a time, I will thank God for you, Dulcinea."

So it is that I again make this first suggestion: devote serious thought to pondering how near and dear to the Father are his suffering children.

My second suggestion is more pointed: an examination of conscience. Does my personal respect for life measure up to my reverence for the Father? Do I react to the foibles and failures of others, or do I respond to the tender Presence that sustains them as it sustains me? We used to say, uncharitably but accurately, of a certain monk, "street angel but house devil." He was wonderful outside the monastery with others, but at home he was hell on wheels. It's possible to consecrate yourself completely to the pro-life position at a meeting and then be anti-life away from the meeting; to pray in the life-giving Spirit of Jesus at the liturgy and act in the death-dealing spirit of the Beast with the Jew next door.

How I treat a brother from day to day, how I react to the sin-scarred wino on the street, how I respond to interruptions from people I dislike, how I deal with normal people in their normal unbelief on a normal day—all this may reveal my reverence or irreverence for the Abba of Jesus more tellingly than the anti-abortion sticker on the bumper of my car.

We're not in favor of life simply because we're warding off death. We're for life because we are for Abba, the essence of all life. And we mature in the wisdom of accepted tenderness to the extent that we stand up for the less fortunate; to the extent that no human flesh is a stranger to us; to the extent that we can touch the hand of another in love; to the extent that for us there truly are no "others."

This is what the world expects from our rhetoric. This is what the world longs to see: men and women who honor the Father by their reverence for life, prophets and lovers aglow with the given tenderness of Jesus' own Spirit, people who live only to love and to reveal love to others. The world craves evidence that the impossible dream is possible, that love exists, that it has a name, that it's the only option for happiness in this world and eternal joy in the next.

If you have a dream, it's *only* a dream; if I have a dream, it remains but a dream. But if we all have the *same* dream, even if it's an impossible dream, it will become reality.

That shared dream is the fruition of Jesus' life, death, and resurrection—the fiery glow of a new Pentecost bursting in the world because of the Spirit-filled tenderness of the Dulcineas and the Men of La Mancha who dream the impossible dream and run where the brave dare not go.

Recommended Reading

Berrigan, Daniel. *Isaiah: Spirit of Courage, Gift of Tears.* Philadelphia: Fortress Press, 1996.

Burghardt, Walter. *Tell the Next Generation, Still Proclaiming Your Wonders, Grace on Crutches, Lovely in Eyes Not His, When Christ Meets Christ.* New York: Paulist Press, 1980, 1984, 1986, 1988, 1993. The late David H. C. Read, pastor of the Madison Avenue Presbyterian Church in New York City, once offered this endorsement: "In my opinion, no one today can equal Walter Burghardt of Georgetown University in expounding the Gospel from the lectionary with clarity, wit, and carefully concealed scholarship."

Cervantes, Miguel. *Don Quixote de la Mancha.* Multiple editions.

Hays, Richard B. *The Moral Vision of the New Testament.* San Francisco: HarperSanFrancisco, 1996.

Shakespeare, William. *The Merchant of Venice.* Multiple editions.

Chapter Five

SIN: THE ENEMY OF TENDERNESS

The fundamental trait of the mature personality in relation to others," writes Adrian van Kaam, "is openness." Openness serves as a bridge to the world of others. It enables us to get involved with others, to understand the thoughts of others, to feel what others are feeling. In other words, if we're open, we're able to enter the existential world of others even if at times we can't identify with someone's particular world. Openness makes us sensitive to any part of the world of others that we can accept and assimilate into our personal universe of faith and thought. Therefore, the mature personality expands in this open communication with a variety of people and their diverse thoughts, feelings, and attitudes.

An early film of Federico Fellini, *La Dolce Vita*, explored the inability of hardened sinners to open themselves to others, their failure to communicate as persons, and their growing callousness through the disappearance of tenderness.

The theme of the film is the decadence of Roman society, the prevalence of sin, and the boredom and ultimate destruction that sin leads to. That theme is given flesh in the progressive deterioration of Marcello, the talented and influential society reporter who lives off the very people he despises and who in the end becomes one of them.

The members of Rome's high society whom we meet in the film try to communicate, but for many of them, communication never manages to penetrate beneath the level of body-sex. *Person* isn't revealed to *person*. By the end of the movie, the viewer senses that the screen is peopled not with persons, but with walking shells within which personality once lived. The failure to communicate strips the characters of all but the last vestiges of humanity.

The first full episode of the film is a nightclub encounter between Marcello and Maddalena, a beautiful, mysterious, and intriguing heiress. In her Cadillac convertible, they drive through the dark streets of Rome, and for a moment it looks as if Maddalena is really trying to understand the attractive man at her side—the one who has too much money encouraging the one who doesn't have enough. Does she see beneath his cool, detached exterior? Is she finally breaking through to his real self? The fledgling intimacy of minds is brought to a sudden halt when she leads him to a basement bed.

Sylvia, a visiting Hollywood star who lights up the film, faithfully mouths for the press the lines she's fed by her publicity agent. But she seems to be more than just a voice and a body. Impulsive, gay, full of impetuous spirits, she enjoys running up the stairs that spiral around the dome of St. Peter's, outdistancing the soft and easily winded photographers. When she reaches the top and gazes out at the *piazza*, she becomes aware of an inner something that responds to the experience. "I can't believe it, I can't believe it," she says, turning to her companion. But he has no eyes for the magnificence; he's leering at her, the international sex symbol.

If only someone could have been there to receive and understand this communication of Sylvia's inner self, someone who could enter into her unique world of thought and feeling and share her vision of Rome—and by sharing quicken the stirrings of her deeper self. But no; spiritually, she's alone.

The final scene of the film is powerful. A young girl, purity personified (who looks, as one critic said, like one of Giotto's angels), beckons from the opposite shore to Marcello, who has just emerged from an orgy of sweet living at a beach house. One sees her lips moving: "Vieni qua, vieni qua"—*Come here, come here.* But he can't quite understand, given the sound of the waves, the inner din of his hangover. He makes a feeble attempt to hear but then shrugs his shoulders—"Non posso sentire"—*I can't hear (and what's more, I can't feel).* And with that he returns to the sweet life like an inmate returning to his cell.

Fellini suggests no antidote for the degeneracy in which his characters live. In the words of one reviewer, "There is no exit from their hell." People isolated from their fellow humans can't survive. Surrounded by non-friends, he becomes a non-man.

To sin, Fellini is saying, is to destroy oneself. Sin becomes its own penalty. Because human nature is spiritual and free, man fulfills himself in actions by which he emerges from egoism to open himself to another. But the ego strives to break down the bridge, closing man in instead of opening him out. Thus, sin always involves some form of self-destruction, for it smothers a man within his own egoism and solitude.

The will no longer guides the sinner's actions by tenderness; egoism fills and obscures his heart. Sin separates man, isolates him. In his communication with others, he no longer has any interest beyond his own benefit or pleasure.

As I realize that I'm reverting to the use of the masculine pronoun exclusively in this chapter, I know intuitively that it's because I'm describing myself. The toll taken by sin over the years, the stunted emotional growth caused by frequent alcoholic relapses, the insensitivity to the feelings of others, the unethical and immoral behavior patterns of dishonesty and deception, the withering of close friendships, the years of spiritual indifference and self-will run riot—all these have shaped a soul that the atheistic existentialist Jean-Paul Sartre described as "en soi et pour soi," *in myself and for myself.*

At this moment of the journey, everything hinges on grace. I can't free myself from self-damnation. I must be set free. Only the fierce mercy of Jesus Christ, which tames the wolves of doubt, shame, and despair, can accomplish my liberation.

Ironically, freedom brings an appreciation for the lessons of captivity: as spiritual genius Anthony de Mello saw with stunning clarity, repentance reaches fullness when we're brought to gratitude for our sins. (More on this in Chapter 7.)

Sin is the starting point of all social estrangement. Every sin, even every sin of thought, leaves its mark on the psychic structure of the human soul. Every unrepented sin has a sinisterly obscuring effect on true openness.

"No man is an island." We need others, every one of us. Human existence is relative; it's what philosopher Martin Heidegger called a "mit-sein," a *being with*. We're social beings by nature. But sin is antisocial; it locks us up in the prison of our own egoism. And that imprisonment bears grave consequences: insofar as we're closed and incommunicative with others, our own personality is impoverished; when we can't reach out to others in a meaningful gesture of love, our own humanity is diminished. Callousness seduces tenderness, and insensitivity becomes a lifestyle.

After every grave sin, something of the power for good is diminished in us. With every subsequent evil act, a measure of our true liberty is destroyed. The freedom to give ourselves to others generously and gently and the readiness to receive are diminished. The daily turning in on self paralyzes our interpersonal exchanges and constitutes a kind of rupture in the evolution of authentic personality. Sin is a closed circuit. Regardless of species, every sin resembles (at least in character) the primal sin of Adam and Eve, which was a closing off from God and one another.

The next time you pause to review your life and examine your conscience, you might find it beneficial for spiritual growth to move beyond the Ten Commandments and address the following questions:

- Have I failed to take the initiative in alleviating fear, anxiety, and heartache in my home, my neighborhood, and the local community?
- Have I had contempt for others: the less educated perhaps, or people of different ethnic, racial, economic, or religious groups?
- Have I dismissed senior citizens as anachronisms and not tried to make them feel their worth and dignity?

- Have I in any way stifled the personal development of another?
- Have I sought to be respected without respecting others?
- Have I often kept others waiting?
- Have I carelessly forgotten (or simply not kept) an appointment or a date?
- Have I been difficult for others to reach, feeling too busy to put myself at their disposal?
- Have I not paid attention when someone is speaking to me?
- Have I kept silent when I should have spoken out?
- Have I responded only to those whose friendship might prove profitable to me?
- Have I blackened the character of anyone by harmful remarks, whether false or true?
- Have I betrayed a trust, violated a confidence, or involved myself in the lives of others through indiscreet words and actions?
- Have I concentrated on what's in it for me rather than what's in me for it?
- Have I failed to appreciate what is because of might-have-beens, should-have-beens, and could-have-beens?

After addressing these issues frankly, ask yourself this crucial final query:

- Having made a dismal response to this set of questions, will I be gentle with myself, as the Master is, humbly acknowledge that the Word hasn't taken sovereign possession of my life, accept my own need for further conversion, quickly repent, ask forgiveness, waste no time in self-recrimination, and smile at my own frailty?

The progressive tendency of sin is to suppress, blind, harden. The following lines from Robert Traver's *Anatomy of a Murder* point up vividly what I'm trying to convey concerning the effects of sin on personality. They're spoken by an old lawyer toward the end of his life:

> [T]he lack of knowledge of people, our lack of human concern with one another, may be the big trouble with this world. For lack of it our world seems to be running down and dying. We now seem fatally bent on communicating with one another only through robot missiles loaded with

cargoes of hate and ruin instead of the human heart with its pent-up cargo of love. And now it seems as though God has finally challenged mankind to open up its heart or perish.

A final word on a substantive issue that the Letter of James commends: "Confess your sins to one another, pray for one another, and this will cure you" (5:16). If we situate sin in its essentially social perspective, we better understand the specific charism of this experience. Confession becomes more than a "Minit-Wash," more than a sigh of relief for summoning the courage and the humility necessary for honest self-disclosure, more than mere satisfaction at having heeded the dictum of James. It becomes a joyful return to the Father's house, a reconciliation with the Christian community in a spirit of atonement and gratitude, a rebuilding of the love-relationship with God and our fellow human beings which sin had attacked, a reopening of the human heart, and a renewed possibility for the full, definitive flowering of the Christian personality in the wisdom of tenderness.

Recommended Reading

Lewis, C. S. *Mere Christianity*. Reprint ed. San Francisco: HarperSanFrancisco, 2001.

Lewis, C. S. *The Screwtape Letters*. Reprint ed. San Francisco: HarperSanFrancisco, 2001.

Manning, Brennan. *Lion and Lamb*. Grand Rapids, MI: Baker Book House, 1986.

Monden, Louis. *Sin, Liberty, and Law*. St. Louis, MO: Herder and Herder, 1962.

Nouwen, Henri J. M. *Compassion: A Reflection on the Christian Life*. New York: Doubleday, 1984.

Wallis, Jim. *The Call to Conversion*. San Francisco: HarperSanFrancisco, 1981.

Chapter Six

Pain and Tenderness

In the course of that night, however, Jacob arose, took his two wives, with the two maidservants and his eleven children, and crossed the ford of the Jabbok. After he had taken them across the stream and had brought over all his possessions, Jacob was left there alone. Then some man wrestled with him until the break of dawn. When the man saw that he would not prevail over him, he struck Jacob's hip at its socket, so that the hip socket was wrenched as they wrestled.

The man then said, "Let me go, for it is day-break." But Jacob said, "I will not let you go until you bless me." "What is your name?" the man asked. He answered, "Jacob." Then the man said, "You shall no longer be spoken of as Jacob, but as Israel, because you have contended with divine and human beings and have prevailed." Jacob then asked him, "Do tell me your name, please." He answered, "Why should you want to know my name?" With that, he bade him farewell. Jacob named the place Peniel. "Because I have seen God face to face," he said, "yet my life has been spared."

Gen. 32:23–31

There's no gentle road to tenderness, as this passage suggests. Tenderness is learned in the testing place, where the man who dares to wrestle with the Absolute limps, and then wins a blessing. Pain is the crucible in which one is made tender. Is it possible that what's true for man is true for God? The Rabbi Heschel passage quoted in Chapter 4 suggests that it is: "There is an old idea in Judaism that God suffers when man suffers. There is a famous text saying that even when a criminal is hanged on the gallows, God cries. God identifies himself with the misery of man."

Does God himself truly love in this way? Does he

get inside our misery and live it through to the point of tender peace? Or does he distance himself from the anguish and agony, the brokenness and pain of the human condition?

Betty Fusco, a housewife from Hollywood, Florida, wrote the following to me in a letter:

One night a young mother who had recently lost her seven-year-old son came to our prayer meeting. Her pain was great. Her hurt and anger were great.

I wonder about this great hurt. This could have been my child. Was he also my child? If not, why am I weeping?

Why, God? Can't you feel our pain? Do you really know how much we hurt?

When Joseph died, what did Mary and Jesus do? Was not their hurt so great that they covered their faces with ashes, cried out in loud voices with weeping and wailing, rent their clothes, and hired mourners to follow the body in the traditional Hebrew fashion of mourning the dead?

And was it in this same Hebrew fashion that on Good Friday, the Father covered his face with ashes—the darkness of midday, the eclipse of the sun?

His earth screamed and groaned in the agony of an earthquake upheaval—the earth trembled and shook—rocks split and mountains fell—he cried out in a loud voice.

He wept—springs burst forth from the splits in the earth; rivers ran wild as their natural courses were changed.

He rent his clothing: the curtain of the sanctuary, the Holy of Holies, the place no one entered, the traditional Hebrew dwelling place of God was torn from top to bottom.

He sent mourners to follow the body. "Tombs opened and many holy men rose from the dead. And after Jesus' resurrection they came forth from the tombs and entered the holy city and appeared to a number of people" (Matt. 27:53).

"Oh yes, Father, you know, for did you not shed tears and intone the lament to show your own deep grief and observe the mourning for a day or two and then were comforted in your sorrow" (Sir. 38:16–18).

For comfort came and comes on Easter morning.

Should you ever visit the cathedral in Fribourg, Switzerland, take note of the third stained-glass window on the right as you enter the church. It depicts the Abba of Jesus standing on Calvary at the foot of the cross with the spit-covered, blood-drenched body of his Son cradled in his arms. The look on the Father's face seems to say, "If I had known what this was going to cost, I never would have permitted it."

Bad theology? Yes. Poor exegesis? Surely. But the artist was not out to theologize or do exegesis. His purpose was to depict in dramatic form the love in the heart of Abba as his beloved Son was slaughtered on that hill outside the city wall of old Jerusalem. We can find truth in poetry, music, Betty Fusco's fresco, and myriad other art forms without getting hung up on the metaphysics of the deity.

Augustine declared, "God is more intimate to me than I am to myself." If God is the personal Ground of Being, intricately connected with all that is, and if God is beyond as well as within our experience of life, love, joy, and pain as we know it, then do we dare to raise the question Where was God in the genocide in Rwanda, the holocaust in Nazi Germany, and the horrific suffering of September 11, 2001? Traditional theology has defended the immutability of God, maintaining that suffering demands change. Since change implies progress toward a higher good, any mutation in the divine nature would indicate an earlier imperfection, and thus makes the notion of a suffering God impossible. While a philosophically based theology endorses such speculation, a suffering God is implicit in a biblically based theology. In the trenchant words of Bonhoeffer, "Only a suffering God can save."

Kevin O'Shea writes,

There is a profound human instinct that God has a heart, that his healing love has demanded that he be incarnate, "hearted," like us. Perhaps the very "heart-dimension" of our existence, if we may call it that, is not something we call our own in an independent sense. Perhaps it is a share in his heart, *a fellowship in his ability to suffer* [italics added]. This may be one reason why the symbol of the tender, redeeming, healing, integrating love of God, given freely in grace, has to be the *Crucified.* He has made peace by the blood of his cross. The opened heart on Calvary is the symbol of the pathos of a healing God. To bear in our heart the openness of that heart is to unfold as a person in the tenderness of given grace.

In the Book of Philippians, Paul states emphatically, "All I want is to know Christ and the power of his resurrection and to share his sufferings by reproducing the pattern of his death" (3:10). The physical suffering in our lives, along with various forms of mental anguish—loneliness, tension, unjust criticism, fear, contradiction and confusion, the inability to relate warmly to others—are among the undramatic life circumstances through which we're formed into the pattern of Christ's death. Likewise, frustration in its myriad forms: in the men and women who long for married life but never achieve it; in those who have a deep desire to become this or that, to accomplish this or that, but in the end have to admit that they lack the necessary gifts; in those who long for friends and companionship but are condemned to loneliness; in those who never seem able to make a success of anything to which they put their hands. In these and countless other life situations, our resemblance to the tenderness of God is realized.

In what sense can we say this? Everybody has a vocation to some form of life-work. However, behind that call (and deeper than any call), everybody has a vocation to be a *person*, to be fully and deeply human in Christ Jesus. And the latter is more important than the former.

It's more important to be a mature Christian than to be a great butcher or baker or candlestick-maker; and if the only chance to achieve the first is to fail at the second, the failure will have proved worthwhile. Isn't failure worthwhile if it teaches us to be gentle with the failure of others, to be patient, to live in the wisdom of accepted tenderness, and to pass that tenderness on to others? If we're always successful, we may get so wrapped up in our own victories that we're insensitive to the anguish of others; we may fail to understand (or even try to understand) the human heart; we may think of success as our due. Then later, if our little world collapses through death or disaster, we have no inner resources.

It's helpful to remember that the value of Jesus' suffering lies not in the pain itself (for, in itself, pain has no value), but in the love that inspired it, as Cyril of

Jerusalem noted long centuries ago. He wrote, "Never forget that what gives value to a sacrifice is not the renouncement it demands but the quality of love which inspired the renouncement." That's exactly how we must approach Calvary. The human soul of Jesus ravished the heart of his heavenly Father with the wild generosity and unflagging obedience of his love.

Fortunately, the cross wasn't the final word that God spoke to his people. Our Christian life looks beyond Calvary to the resurrection. It's the human nature of the risen Christ, shot through and through with the radiance of divinity, that shows like a brilliant mirror all that we're summoned to. The fate of Christ our brother is our own fate. If we've suffered with him, we shall be glorified with him.

The pattern is always the same. All roads lead to Calvary. We reach life only through death; we learn tenderness only through pain; we come to light only through darkness; Jonah must be buried in the whale's belly; the grain of wheat must die; we must be formed into the pattern of his death if we are to become Easter men and Easter women.

Recommended Reading

Bonhoeffer, Dietrich. *The Cost of Discipleship.* New York: Touchstone, 1959.

O'Shea, Kevin. *The Way of Tenderness.* New York: Paulist Press, 1978.

Stella, Tom. *The God Instinct.* Notre Dame, IN: Sorin Books, 2001.

Chapter Seven

FIERCE MERCY

The three parables of divine mercy in Luke 15, often called "the Gospel within the Gospel," carry the central message of Jesus Christ. The stories of the lost sheep, the lost coin, and the lost son pummel our conscience into submission to the saving truth that God is love (1 John 4:16). Biblical scholar William Shannon argues that this portion of the Bible is hermeneutically decisive, meaning that it's the key for understanding everything else in Scripture.

Let's meditate on the first of these three parables and ask the Spirit to lead us into the mystery of divine mercy.

Irrationally, the shepherd has left ninety-nine of his flock in the desert, where danger lurks and wild beasts roam, to search out little guy lost. When he finds the lost one, he hoists him on his shoulders and merrily goes home. Spiritual writer Eddie Ensley, in his book *Prayer That Heals Our Emotions,* encourages us to envision that scene:

Imagine that you are the shepherd. You leave the flock to hunt the lone frightened lamb that has lost its way and is now on a cliff high on a hill, frightened to come down on its own. The lamb is crying out as though for its mother. You can hear the desperation in that cry. You soothe and stroke the lamb. You speak soft words and you see the lamb's muscles loosen up and calmness return. The lamb nuzzles you with its head. You pick up the lamb and put it on your shoulder. What are your feelings? A scene like this is one of tenderness, of warmth, of compassion, of joy. Allow yourself to feel the tenderness of the lamb on your neck as you bring it back.

Tenderness, warmth, compassion. With elements such as these, this parable and its two companions are decidedly "un-American." As a tragic consequence, they barely register on the contemporary Christian psyche. How do I know this? Throughout almost forty years of pastoral experience, I've observed disciples of Jesus badger, bully, and bludgeon themselves into earning God's mercy. The haunting memories of failed relationships, callous disregard of children, sexual peccadilloes, financial indiscretions, words of love not spoken, support not offered, compassion not extended, and abysmal indifference to human need suddenly resurface, sometimes from decades past. These unwanted recollections paralyze faith, overwhelm the message of Jesus, and often lead to drug-induced states of consciousness, providing the temporary escape from shame and blame.

A virulent strain of Pelagian theology courses through the stream of spiritual consciousness in the United States. Pelagius taught that people are basically good—untainted by original sin and in control of their destiny. Today this corrupt theology is fueled by madly diligent efforts in the workplace marshaled to reap the prescribed rewards of the technological juggernaut. Recently, during dinner on a Saturday night in Kirkland, Washington, a small town close to Microsoft headquarters, six young couples, after scarfing down their food, abruptly left the restaurant at nine. I said to my host,

"That's strange! It's Saturday night." He replied, "Actually, it's pretty common around here. They're probably going back to work at Gates/World. They'll all be millionaires before they hit their thirtieth birthday."

A culture that prizes effort and reward simply transfers the Horatio Alger legend of the self-made man from the economic sphere to our relationship with God. The notion of unmerited mercy is quaint but unintelligible to most of us, since it has no prototype in our human experience. The dramatic surprise that comes in the stories of the searching shepherd, the searching woman, and the searching father is that being found by a searching God is more important than anything we do. If the message fails to resonate within us, we can't fault the messenger.

In my own life, the transition from tenderness to mercy developed through a ruthless examination of conscience—or, as recovering alcoholics put it, through a searching and fearless moral inventory of myself. The results were chilling.

All the ministerial successes of previous years were weighed and found wanting. Base but well-disguised motives contaminated almost every act of kindness that I did. In the light of that sickening discovery, the feeling of being comfortably close to the Abba of Jesus disappeared, like last night's dream. No longer sheltered by the loving awareness of God's presence, I felt a vast chasm suddenly open, separating me, in my calculated dishonesty, from the pure truth of God. A vague and pervasive sense of existential guilt crept into my soul.

Remorse over the past invaded my soul with such uncompromising cruelty that I became afraid of myself. I stayed in bed until noon, walked unsteadily into the den, and never opened the Venetian blinds. Light was unbearable. In a harrowing vision I saw my alleged virtues as spiritually glamorous vices, everything vitiated by self-seeking. I had toyed with people's emotions, indulged in sarcasm when I could have affirmed a brother or sister, bruised when I could have healed through a word of consolation, bitten when I could have kissed. My whole life seemed like a lie. I had used my God-given gifts to build a career out of religion, to forge an empire, to capture the allegiance of the crowds. The deadening words, phony, fraud, and hypocrite sounded and resounded in my hollow heart, followed by moments of nausea at my vanity and falsity. The authenticity of my whole life-project seemed doomed.

A former professor of mine at Columbia University, Quentin Anderson, once said, "We must gather round the sacred fire of community life." Those words now struck me as a cruel hoax. The community had nothing to offer me; no one had a word that could take away my emptiness. It would be futile to search frantically for a key, a formula, a program of things to do in order to find my way back to the lost paradise of closeness with God. In the brokenness of my given situation, I was outside any healing. No one could present me with a remedy. Tenderness was gone.

In that hour of loss, I felt so far from God that I doubted whether a whole lifetime would be long enough to find him. I suspected that my life had been a major disappointment to God, a disappointment that I was powerless to undo. I had lost the Lord through a pride that had blinded me and a harshness that had hardened my heart. Utterly desperate, I convinced myself that the rebuke of the judge in the Book of Revelation was spoken with me in mind: "You're stale. You're stagnant. You make me want to vomit. You brag, 'I'm rich, I've got it made, I need nothing from anyone,' oblivious that in fact you're a pitiful, blind beggar, threadbare and homeless" (Rev. 3:16–17, *The Message*).

In the vividly remembered past, my life and ministry had occasioned paeans of praise. I had made my mark; I had produced good work; I had been respected and esteemed by my peers. It seemed that my integrity had given me a lasting claim to a security of sorts. But now the success of earlier years was riddled with ambiguity and arrogance. Friendships and popularity waned as relapses with alcohol were brushed aside and ignored. Personal stories that placed me in a flattering light were grossly exaggerated. I became aware of distrust on the part of others and of radical differences of opinion regarding liturgy, spiritual renewal, and community life. Illness, burnout, and inactivity exacerbated the shame of buried memories that refused to stay interred.

In a frazzled emotional state, I became conscious of a growing estrangement from my own self as well. Looking in the mirror, I saw only the husk in which someone real used to live and grow. Then a flashback: years earlier, I had been offered the position of campus minister at a prestigious university. Without a moment's hesitation, I had answered, "That won't be possible. The ministry of evangelization is my foremost priority and demands a full-time commitment." Who said that?

Who was that flippant self who decided that my gift of inspired speech was so indispensable to the life of the church? At what unremembered moment did I start taking myself so seriously?

Kevin O'Shea, in *The Thorn and the Rose,* describes poignantly the numbness induced by estrangement from self:

> It is not a hell, it is just an eternal limbo . . . condemned to an eternal waiting in the alien ground of the self, that no one can recognize and no one can tread except the self encaptured within it. It is the impossible point between any hope and all despair, untouchable because it is neither. It is a numbness in the roots of one's being. It is a real saying, "I am not." . . . The feeling is bitter, but the sense of bitterness has died. . . . And the existence is known in something one could never have called an "experience."

Trembling anxiety emptied my heart of any desire for an experience of God's presence. His holiness was unbearable. The mere thought of Christ was painful and fearful; he was the opposite of my own being, the enemy of my infidelity. Solitary, lonely, incommunicative, lost, I saw God as *mysterium tremendum*—Rudolph Otto's phrase for that sense of tremendous mystery that's the deepest and most fundamental element in all spiritual experience. God was totally Other, majestic, fear-inspiring, everything I was not. I knew the passage, "It's a terrible thing to fall into the hands of the living God," was aimed directly at me; the prospect of divine judgment filled me with terror. The contrast between my sinfulness and God's holiness allowed only the desperate prayer of the tax collector, "O God, have mercy on me, a sinner," I prayed these words over and over and over.

The acceptance of mercy was no longer one option among many. Utter spiritual exhaustion had lowered my every defense mechanism, just as clinical depression depletes every ounce of energy in the stricken person. In the depths of my own woundedness, I knew that there had to be a moment when I simply let go. I was bleeding in my heart, and I couldn't stop the hemorrhaging.

When mercy stole quietly into my soul, the trembling stopped and the tears—which in my self-estrangement had dried up—began to flow again. The touch of infinite kindness to my nothingness wasn't mere tenderness; it was suffused with a gentleness that transcended tenderness. And yet the experience was so subtle that mercy entered my heart unnoticed.

The shabby streets of my soul were still littered with the debris of vanity, dishonesty, and degraded love. It wasn't as if a sanitation worker had suddenly appeared to rid the neighborhood of every mound of unsightly garbage. When mercy came in the back door, my character defects didn't bolt out the front door; they went underground, but they didn't leave (and still haven't). What happened is virtually impossible to explain—and it's the better for that. What I intuitively apprehend now, in retrospect, is that mercy kissed my brokenness, Too-Much-Love (John 3:16) cradled a wounded child, and for a biblically valid but inexplicable reason it was okay to be bent.

Later and farther down the road, the first act of the merciful love of God within me was to shred the illusions and delusions that had led me to deny my own worth and attempt to eliminate the life of the Spirit of God within me. My erratic mind had unleashed a series of symbols and inner images, at times irrational and uncontrollable, that fed an irremediable guilt I was powerless to expiate. It was only when the dreadful thought that bad faith would inevitably return to disfigure my life anew that fierce mercy burst into my consciousness with a feral protectiveness: "You belong to me, and no one will ever snatch you from my hand. I have changed your name. No longer shall you be called ashamed, guilt-ridden, lonely, and much-afraid. Your new name is 'child of mine, broken and beloved, playful one and joy of my heart.'"

When fierce mercy transforms our lives, the bewildering words of Julian of Norwich, "Sin will be no shame but honor," become luminously clear, as does the baffling observation of the spiritual genius Anthony deMello, "Repentance reaches fullness when you are brought to gratitude for your sins."

God's glory is to forgive. As the prophet Micah exclaims to Yahweh, "What god can compare with you: taking fault away, pardoning crime, not cherishing anger forever but delighting in showing mercy" (7:18). It is effortless for God to forgive. God delights in forgiveness, because his forgiveness generates new life in us. The incomparable joy of the prodigal's father in the "pearl of the parables" would have been denied if his youngest son had always been a goody-two-shoes.

Our sins are carriers of grace when they lead to repentance and authentic contrition. Like the prodigal son, we come to know an intimacy with the Father that the sinless, self-righteous brother never knew. For the sins that brought us to this sacred intimacy, we are indeed grateful. They provide the opportunity for God to show mercy, which the Hebrew and Christian Scriptures testify is his greatest delight. German theologian Werner Bergengruen states it precisely: "Love proves its authenticity in fidelity, but reaches its completion in forgiveness." Small wonder that Too-Much-Love finds such excessive joy in mercy.

In reply to the frivolous question "Then why not keep sinning?" ask the prodigal son, after he's experienced the depths of his father's love, "Do you plan another safari into depravity?" Ask the husband whose wife has just told him, "I love you so deeply that nothing, absolutely nothing, could ever destroy the love I have for you; nothing could ever make me stop loving you," whether he feels free to embark on an affair. Love calls forth love!

The omnipresent temptation of the superficial soul is to pretend that we're sinners and to pretend we're forgiven—it's all pretense because the sins we acknowledge are not those that decimate us, and the forgiveness we claim is sham because of our flagrant dishonesty with God and each other. The spiritual life becomes a carnival sideshow of pseudo-repentance and pseudo-peace. However, when the scourge of sin rips our life apart and the rawness of our spirit longs for the sweet salve of relief, we may stagnate between choosing to endure the shame or choosing to trust mercy and to internalize Julian's words, "Our courteous Lord does not want his servants to despair because they fall often and grievously; for our falling does not hinder him in loving us." The grace for the latter choice is not denied to anyone "who cries out to him day and night, even when he delays to help them" (Luke 18:7).

The Word that can save us isn't our own word; salvation doesn't depend on any residual capacity for good within us. What saves us is the living Word of Too-Much-Mercy (Luke 1:77–78), who draws life out of death, perfection out of disaster, and self-forgiveness out of self-condemnation.

"Blessed are the merciful: they shall have mercy shown them," Jesus promises (Matt. 5:7). If we attend with perseverance to our own sorry story, we're not only disinclined to judge others peremptorily; we're also well-disposed to extend mercy indiscriminately to the rogues and ragamuffins whom God places on our path. Note Simon Tugwell's astringent observation: "We can only receive mercy if we are prepared to accept the company that Mercy places us in. It is no good wanting to be shown mercy and then reserving the right to look on disapprovingly at all the other fellows."

Since *receiving* mercy is inseparable from *showing* mercy, unceasing prayer must include the cry to turn my heart of stone into a heart of flesh. We all stand in urgent need of the same mercy, but showing mercy to others isn't an easy option, especially when it comes to lavishing benevolence on ingrates who have no intention of reform. Yet that's what Abba does. "He himself is kind to the ungrateful and the wicked" (Luke 6:35). Moreover, my own complicity in evil is manifested in my self-justifying resistance to expressing any genuine warmth to someone who has hurt me; I'm trapped in the same web of wretchedness the transgressor is. Clearly, the tender heart isn't made of putty.

All the great experiences of life—the freedom to be, our encounters with truth, loving and being loved, daily dying to self, and so forth—are worked out in the quiet turbulence of an impoverished spirit. A gentleness that transcends tenderness comes over us when we confront decisive moments involving these experiences, and we're quietly but deeply moved by that indescribable encounter with mercy. As we're overtaken by the overpowering force of mystery, we suddenly become little. We can no longer come at God with our unwarranted professionalism or our obnoxious familiarity, and we know it. We would be neither surprised nor shocked if God walked in and blew our entire meditation to itsy-bitsies.

As we draw near to our wellspring, our thoughts become devout, our understanding mellows, our words slacken, our judgment becomes reserved, and our objectivity gains reverence. How do we deal with this wordless, empty, but shattering collision with the Ground of Being—of our being? Why this withdrawal from the cozy fireplace of tender colloquies and hand-clapping liturgies into the relentless poverty of a deep, chilling stillness that invades the inner sanctum of our being?

According to Rudolph Otto, the reason is *mysterium tremendum*, that sense of tremendous mystery that surrounds our every thought of God, our every prayer to him. Beyond faith, trust, love, peace, and joy, we sense an element of bewildering strength—a strength so great that it would be humanly impossible for us to create, invent, or manufacture such an experience. For one person it may come sweeping like a gentle but relentless tide, saturating the mind and heart in a self-forgetting spirit of profound worship. For another, it may linger and embed itself in an enduring mode that's resonant with awe and wonder, until at last it fades away and the believer returns to the normal routine of everyday existence. As one contemplative humorously phrased it, "After the ecstasy, the laundry!"

At other times, the force of *mysterium tremendum* may erupt like a volcano, surging up from the depths of the soul in spasms and convulsions. It may lead to intoxicated frenzy such as that experienced by the sixteenth-century mystic Philip Neri, who would press his hands with all his might against the walls to forestall spiritual inebriation, levitation, or ecstasy. At still other times, the force of *mysterium tremendum* may become the hushed trembling and speechless humility of C. S. Lewis, who was "surprised by joy." Whatever the nature of the experience, we stand in the presence

of mystery inexpressible, above all creatures and beyond all telling.

It is the decisive inbreak of God into our personal
history, the transforming moment when tenderness is
no longer congruent with our perception of reality; the
felt intimacy of a bygone faith is inappropriate to the
present parameters of spiritual experience; "Abba,"
"beloved Father," "brother Jesus," and "gentle Spirit"
have become dry words, vacant images that resonate no
more in the inner sanctum of our heart. Those words
and images have served their purpose as anthropomor-
phic pointers to the reality of Too-Much-Love that lies
beyond, and tenderness is redefined as mercy.

When that moment of truth arrives we no longer
have any resources to resist the imperious summons of
mystery, no credentials of independence to flash. The
moment of truth has arrived.

As German theologian Johannes Metz writes,
"Worshipping in spirit and truth (John 4:23), we no
longer bear ourselves with the swagger of the executive
who knows what is up and has all under his control. . . .
We are mistaken, however, if we expect to find in prayer
a shelter from the overwhelming force of mystery."

While prayer is our natural response to any encounter with ultimate mystery, James Mulholland
reminds us that not just any prayer will do. If we forget
who it is to whom we're praying—forget the power with
which we're dealing—we approach the Holy One as
Santa Claus, supplying God with a to-do list, burying
awe and wonder beneath a flurry of petitions, and gain-
ing from our tithing, fasting, and devotional life a sense
of entitlement to an immediate divine response. Most
curious of all, Jesus is conspicuously absent from the
pre-Christian prayer of Jabez and similar invocations.

When we deny our inherent spiritual poverty, when
we get too affluently involved with ourselves, danger
lurks. We may begin to make demands on God for
things that we think we deserve, often leading to anger
and frustration. Classic case: Man in restaurant orders
crabmeat salad and the server brings shrimp salad.
Livid, angry man roars, "Where the hell's my crabmeat?" If we presume that life owes us the best—and
nothing but the best—then reality rarely lives up to our
expectations.

What follows logically is that we blithely take for
granted everything that comes our way. The spiritually
poor—like the economically poor—experience genuine

gratitude and appreciate the slightest gift. Ironically, the more we grow in the Spirit of Jesus Christ, the poorer we become. The more we realize that everything is gift, the more the tenor of our life becomes one of humble, joyful thanksgiving.

The rich in spirit devote considerable time to thinking about what they *don't* have; the poor get right down to enjoying and celebrating what they *do* have. In the nineteenth century, the atheist philosopher Friedrich Nietzsche reproached a group of Christians. "You make me sick!" was the gist of his complaint. When their spokesman asked why, Nietzsche replied, "Because you redeemed don't look like you're redeemed!" The rich in spirit are often as downcast, guilt-ridden, anxious, and dissatisfied as their unbelieving neighbors, while the poor cry, "It is right to give God thanks and praise!"

So how do we get from the poverty of spiritual wealth to the wealth of spiritual poverty? The prayer of quiet regard, liberation from inordinate self-consciousness, and attention to the attentiveness of Jesus reveal the unfathomable depths of our poverty. In the awareness of our radical dependence, the illusion of self-sufficiency melts away like the morning mist.

We're so poor that not even our poverty is our own; it belongs to the *mysterium tremendum* of God. In prayer we drink the dregs of our poverty, professing the plenitude and majesty of Someone else. The ultimate word of the poor in spirit is, "Not I, and not Thou, not one and not two," but the singer and the song, the flame and the fire. The impoverished ragamuffin drains the cup when he disappears into what Thomas Merton called "the tremendous poverty that is the adoration of God." He stands before God with open hands, not clinging to anything.

No longer enslaved to the tyranny of peak religious experiences of the past, the poor in spirit abandon the desperate search to recapture the prayerful intimacy of tenderness. Tom Stella tells the story of one of his visits to Genesee Abbey in upper New York. He asked a monk who had been there for thirty years whether the man experienced a sense of God's closeness more at that point than when he first entered the monastery. "Expecting an affirmative response," says Stella, "I was both surprised and consoled when he said, 'No, but now it doesn't matter.'" Mercifully, the certainty of faith in the indwelling Presence doesn't depend on the rise and fall of our fickle feelings.

God is God. The Holy One isn't to be commanded, controlled, manipulated, or exploited.

The apostle Paul asks, "Does something molded say to the molder, 'Why did you make me like this?'" (Rom. 9:20). When we accept that truth, we realize that times of worship can no longer be evaluated by the felt effects they produce in us; the quality of the eucharistic meal can't be measured by the number of chairs at the table, the nature of the appetizers, or the tangible, visible results on a diner's psyche. The poor are bewildered that mercy has even bothered to show up, nonplussed that God and man at table are sat down.

When we're brought face to face with the inescapable poverty of death, the gradual movement from living in the wisdom of tenderness to living in the presence of mercy becomes decisive and complete. The awesome reality of *mysterium tremendum* stakes its sovereign claim. "At this point," notes Johannes Metz, "poverty comes to full achievement. Submission to the forces of one's death-bound nature becomes obedient self-abandonment to the Father."

Twenty-five years ago, a friend of mine in Florida learned that she was dying. As her last will and testament, Edith Dinan wrote the following:

When this earthly body of mine is quiet and breathes no more, make a joyful noise unto the Lord, my friends. Do not weep unless you weep for yourselves; do not weep for me. Instead, dance and sing and shout the Good News—another child has gone home to the Father, Abba.

Sing songs of joy late into the night and, if there are hardy ones among you, sing and praise and play and laugh into the dawn; then let the Mass be a celebration of true happiness and joy. Give praise to God, for He is mercy! He has called me home.

Sorrow not, dear friends, on my going, but be glad. Think of me kindly and often if you wish, but only with delight and joy.

Let not the celebration of my true birth into the Lord be a humdrum thing, but let the halls ring with gladness and mirth! Praise our God, for He is good! He has called me home and I go with love, expectation, and praise on my lips and joy in my heart. . . . In my absolute knowledge that I am a Beloved of the Father, a bride of Christ, and a temple of the Holy Spirit, I write this as my last will and testament. If you love me, please be filled with joy and do what I ask.

Edith is already in the Kingdom, of course, for as Leon Bloy writes, "You do not enter paradise tomorrow or ten years from tomorrow; you enter paradise today, when you are poor and crucified."

Death is the last act of self-giving, the final repudiation of self, the ultimate act of impoverished ragamuffins before the fierce mercy of God. In unshaken trust, unwavering hope, and the pure giving of love, we hand over the kingdom of ourselves to the Father. And the Abba of Jesus, standing on the eternal shores with open, outstretched arms, gently beckons us home, saying,

> *Come now, my love, my lovely one, come,*
> *For you the winter is past,*
> *The snows are over and gone.*
> *The flowers appear in the land,*
> *The season of joyful songs has come.*
> *The cooing of the turtle dove is heard in our land. . . .*
> *Come now, my love, my lovely one, come, . . .*

Let me see your face,

Let me hear your voice.

For your voice is sweet

And your face so beautiful.

Come now, my love, my lovely one, come.

Song of Sol. 2:10–14

Recommended Reading

Bergengruen, Werner. Quoted in *The God Who Won't Let Go.* Cincinnati, OH: Ave Maria Press, 2001.

Ensley, Eddie. *Prayer That Heals Our Emotions.* San Francisco: HarperSanFrancisco, 1988.

Julian of Norwich. *Showings.* New York: Paulist Press, 1980.

Metz, Johannes. *Poverty of Spirit.* New York: Paulist Press, 1968.

Mulholland, James. *Praying Like Jesus.* San Francisco: HarperSanFrancisco, 2001.

√ O'Shea, Kevin. *The Thorn and the Rose.* New York: Paulist Press, 1978.

Otto, Rudolph. *The Idea of the Holy.* New York: Scribner, 1927.

Shannon, William. *Silence on Fire.* New York: Crossroad, 1991.

Tugwell, Simon. *The Beatitudes: Soundings in Christian Tradition.* Springfield, IL: Templegate, 1980.

A Word
After . . .

Loyal, tender-hearted shepherds respond to the gentle Presence that sustains their brothers and sisters in the human family. However, when the dignity of others is trampled by the machinations of political or religious leaders, they're not afraid to stand up for the truth and sustain the disapproval of the power-brokers. They're incapable of remaining silent in the face of flagrant injustice. They heed the words inscribed on the tabernacle of a village church, "The greatest thing on earth is respect, because it is the heart of love." If speaking and acting on behalf of the marginalized is the only alternative, tender-hearted Christians become confrontational, angry, and unrelenting;

should circumstances demand, they're wild and woolly adversaries.

These observations serve as a short preface to this last word.

If Christian imagination, long mummified within the legalisms and barbarisms of a soulless church, suddenly quickened, like the snap of a switchblade, it might create an image of the unimaginable: a unified Christian community in America!

Imagination focused on Jesus and anchored in his Word liberates us from the tyranny of the existing arrangement; unglues us from the stuckness of the status quo; unlocks closed doors so that we can look anew at Torah, Christ, church, and cosmos; implies that I can be more than I am at any given moment; and promises that the epitaph on my tombstone will read more than, "He muttered his prayers, mowed his lawn, and lost a thousand golf balls."

An exercise: Let's imagine that the apostle Paul, who lived the words he wrote in Second Corinthians, "The Lord is the Spirit, and where the Spirit of the Lord is, there is freedom" (3:17), has been given a crash course in the English language and transported via a time machine into the present. It's a Sunday afternoon in New Orleans, and Paul is hungry. He buys a shrimp po'boy from a Chartres Street vendor and, heeding his advice to Timothy, purchases a California wine-cooler. He crosses to the Moonwalk on Decatur Street, reaches the top step, and gets his first view of the Mississippi River. Then he seats himself on a wooden bench next to a white-haired gentleman.

"Good day, sir," Paul says, pulling the po'boy from his bag. "Perhaps you could share with me your perspective on the spiritual state of the Christian community in America today?"

The man turns and coolly appraises the stranger. He sees a man of small stature with a large nose, sparse red hair, well-formed chin, gray eyes under thick joined eyebrows, and a heavy beard. *Who is this guy?* the man wonders. *A media mole digging for dirt, a dilettante dabbling in spiritual things, the enemy disguised as an angel of light?*

"Why do you ask?" he says skeptically.

Paul takes a swig from his wine-cooler, thinking through his response. Then he says, "A disciple of your era wrote, 'Many Christians have gathered like ravens around the carcass of cheap grace and there have drunk the poison which has killed the following of Christ.' If

seekers are to encounter Jesus today, they must find
him in his body, the Christian community. I ask, sir,
because I want to meet Jesus on your turf."

The older man, clad in jeans, turtleneck, and Ree-
boks, listens intently. His eyes never leave Paul's face.
*This inconspicuous little fellow emanates an unquestionable
spiritual force, he thinks. Yet his appearance, gestures, and
voice don't fit the picture of conventional piety. He seems
neither worldly nor mystical. He doesn't have the riveting,
unflinching stare of the "born-again" crowd—a stare that
often suggests a neurotic condition masquerading as sinceri-
ty. And he hasn't come after me with one sledgehammer
blow of the Bible after another. Obviously, he's read
Bonhoeffer, though; he quoted him.*

*And the honesty in his eyes is unmistakable. I've lis-
tened to a number of preachers,* the Reebok man mused,
*who have mesmerized me with spellbinding oratory inter-
laced with a self-deprecating humor designed to create the
impression that they're humble, but something in their eyes
gives them away. A barely perceptible movement of the iris
tells me that many preachers inhabit a vacant part of their
mind. They've so polished and repolished their style over
the years that they've forgotten the substance of their mes-*

sage and speak simply for the sake of speaking. Contrived passion, artificial fire. The eyes betray the rhetoric. I remember meeting a farmer who got so animated about his potato crop that he was more credible than the typical preacher. It's all in the eyes! The same is true of this stranger sitting next to me. I'm forced to take him seriously because of his gaze.

The Reebok man stands decisively and holds out his hand. "My name is Daniel," he says. "Let's take a walk."

Paul shakes hands warmly and offers his first name in return. He puts his empty bottle into his bag, along with his sandwich wrapping, and tosses everything into a nearby trash can. Then the men set off.

"My brother," Daniel begins, "I can't remember a time when the name of Jesus Christ has been invoked more often than now, or the content of his teaching been so thoroughly ignored. His words have been twisted, spindled, and mutilated to mean anything, everything, and nothing. The seduction of cheap grace has created mass-market, cost-free discipleship. By and large, Americans are spoonfed on the pabulum of popular religion.

"Academically, many professors of religion have turned Christianity into the religion of the professors. They speak to one another in pedantic tones of the soteriological value of Jesus' suffering and death, write learned papers in dreary prose, finesse the exegesis of biblical passages, split hairs over hermeneutical principles, authoritatively announce, 'Jesus said this but didn't say that,' and seldom relate the Word of God to the needs of the Christian community. The esoteric language of many religion scholars makes their work inaccessible to the average layperson. Yet Bible studies proliferate, often at the expense of authentic Christian conduct.

"What Martin Luther and other reformers learned from the apostle Paul, who advised us 'to know nothing except Jesus Christ and him crucified,' has been usurped by the gifts of the Holy Spirit, including praying in tongues and private revelations of doubtful authenticity. The staple of the typical Sunday sermon is heavy-handed moralizing tinged with raw emotional appeal that lays guilt on the people and breeds fear, shame, and distorted images of God. For many devout people who hear such sermons, the Good News isn't news and it isn't good.

"Paul, another issue bewitching God's people these days is the tendency to gratuitously give a monopoly on evil to a single person (such as Osama bin Laden), a single nation (such as Afghanistan), or a single institution (be it Islam, Judaism, the Mormon Church, or the Catholic Church).

"When one person, nation, or institution is declared to be Satan, logic rules: eliminate this source of all evil, and everything will be all right; when Satan is localized in a finite reality, the end of evildoing is just around the corner.

"And yet, as you know, brother, one lesson we've learned from the history of civilized humanity is that when we kill our particular 'Satan,' evil doesn't disappear from the face of the earth. In fact, it may reappear in the place we least suspect: ourselves. Remember the movie *Ben-Hur?* When Judah finally kills Massala—his 'Satan'—Judah's lover turns to him and says, 'It is as if you have become Massala.'

"Labeling someone Satan gets the labeler off the hook. The source of evil has a specific face and shape (and it's surely not I!).

"Here's the problem, Paul. Many Christians today have discerned the speck in the eye of another, and they think they need look no further. Everyone has a pet peeve, a favorite target, a personalized 'what's wrong with the world' speech. The villain may be televangelists, racism, the welfare system, the immigration system, the worldliness of the church—whatever. No one of us is immune from spreading evil, including those who pontificate about what the *real* problem is.

"Brother Paul, American Christians revel in this kind of declamation. The tragedy is that the scorching words of Jesus in Matthew 23, 'Woe to you scribes and Pharisees, you hypocrites,' are now directed at other churches, authority figures such as the pope, the presiding bishop, politicians of the opposing party, the ACLU, and so forth. You and I know that we miss Jesus' message entirely when we use his fierce words against anyone other than ourselves. Those words must be understood as directed to the self; otherwise, they're perverted.

"And that, Paul, is the form, shape, and stuff of Christian pharisaism today. Hypocrisy isn't the prerogative of people in high places. It's the natural expression of what's meanest in us all."

Daniel looks over at Paul and notices how intently he's listening. It's not the riveted concentration of knitted eyebrows but the quietness of pure attention. "This is getting heavy, brother," he says. "Shall I continue, or would you like to take a break?"

"Please go on," Paul says encouragingly, "but let's sit down on the embankment."

They seat themselves comfortably on the grass, and twenty minutes of silence follow. Daniel has more to say, but he isn't sure how to proceed, and Paul is immersed in thought.

Finally Paul says, "Faith comes through hearing. Are people not hearing the Word of God today?"

"Well, yes and no," Daniel replies. "As you recall, I said earlier that professors of religion have turned Christianity into the religion of the professors. The supreme irony is that ministers of the gospel have twisted the Word into the gospel of the ministers. Not *all* ministers, of course, or all professors. There are many who preach what Jesus preached and teach what Jesus taught. Their sermons brim with purity and power. Alas, though, the majority of them ignore the Great Commandment and unleash their anger on those who challenge their doctrine or fail to interpret the Scriptures as they do.

"A classic case in point: The teaching of Jesus on the indissolubility of marriage is unbending and uncompromising. Yet the apostle Paul, who arguably understood the mind of Christ better than anyone before or since his time, didn't hesitate to intervene in the unhappy marriage of a believer yoked to an unbeliever. Invoking his own apostolic authority, Paul modified the teaching of Jesus and dissolved the marriage, because—as he wrote in his Letter to the Romans—'God has called us to a life of peace.' And elsewhere he said, 'We have the mind of Christ.'

"Paul, the only effective foundation for nationwide Christian renewal lies in attaining Christ-consciousness, in moving beyond the bare letter of the Bible into the God-consciousness of Jesus. The major cause of division and darkness in the American church is our failure to achieve the mind of Christ. Rigidity rules, and the freedom of Christ has been obscured. Tenderness has vanished. A scrupulous moral code substitutes for an engaged, participatory encounter with the Master. The result is a religion about Jesus and not the religion of Jesus.

"The violence with which some Christians expound their beliefs makes me think that they're trying to convince themselves. The specter of their well-concealed unbelief frightens them, so they become more militant and strident. When this same fear grips the churches, they disintegrate into lifeless propagators of formal rituals or intolerant agents of repression. Without an intimate, heartfelt knowledge of Jesus, the preachers who staff these churches resemble travel agents handing out brochures to places they've never visited.

"The consequences of such ignorance have proved disastrous, Paul. Rampant legalism has a stranglehold on a significant section of the evangelical arm of the American church. Fear has gained such a foothold that it's assumed to be a normal part of Christian life."

Daniel heaves a heartfelt sigh. "Have you ever heard of a group called the National Guild of Christian Therapists?" he asks.

"No," says Paul, shaking his head. "My attention has been elsewhere. Are they trustworthy?"

"More than that, they're credible and committed. In their latest report, they narrate the widespread phenomenon of clients tormented by intense feelings of guilt, shame, remorse, and self-punishment. They've concluded that these things are the dominant symptoms of a psycho/spiritual sickness afflicting American Christians today: the bitter fruits of legalism, perfectionism, and guilt-tripping don't fall far from the tree. Many of the clergy and laity thrash about trying to fix themselves, improve their prayer life, make themselves presentable to God and lovable to others. Sooner rather than later, they're appalled by their inconsistency, dejected by their mediocrity, and depressed because they haven't met their own lofty expectations. In the self-help spiritual swamp, there are no survivors.

"One last observation, if you can bear with me, Paul. The greatest single need in the church today is to know Jesus Christ through engaged, participatory encounter. When religion replaces the actual experience of the living Jesus, when we lose the authority of personal knowing and rely on the authority of books, institutions, and leaders, when we let religion interpose between us and the primary experience of Jesus as the Christ, we lose the very reality that religion itself describes as ultimate. Therein lies the origin of all holy wars, bigotry, intolerance, and division within the body of Christ.

"Brother Paul, I've spoken at great length. Pray for

me that I have the courage to stand fast and love the brethren in their brokenness."

Paul rises quickly to his feet. "Daniel, the range and depth of your insight into the contemporary church is remarkable," he says. "How is it that you're so knowledgeable?"

"I'm a bishop," says Daniel, also rising. "Two years ago, I was appointed by the elders of the National Assembly of American Churches to freelance the country as a pastor/theologian-at-large. This week I'm to report my findings and to make recommendations for reform and renewal. Frankly, I'm at a loss. The task is overwhelming."

Paul grabs the older man's arm. "Would it be possible for you to convene an emergency meeting of the elders tomorrow night?" he asks. "I wish to speak to them."

Daniel eyes him skeptically. "You what?"

"I wish to address a prophetic word to the National Assembly."

"Who *are* you?"

"As I told you earlier, my name is Paul. These are my credentials." Paul strips off his shirt. "The brand marks on my body are those of Jesus. I'm an apostle who doesn't owe his authority or his appointment to any man. I was appointed by the Father, who raised Jesus from the dead. My only boast is the cross of Christ, which has set me free from the tyranny of pleasing others and conforming to the petty patterns they dictate. As you can see, I bear on my body the signature of Jesus. Will you arrange the meeting?"

Daniel nods his head in affirmation. "Tomorrow night in the grand ballroom of the Corinthian Hotel," he says.

The two separate in silence.

The following night fifteen hundred elders gather from every region of the country—pastors, evangelists, superintendents, bishops, cardinals, primates, prelates, provincials, archimandrites, generals, and untitled shepherds. Some come robed and bearded, others are in three-piece suits, many are in clerical collars, and a minority sport T-shirts and jeans. Murmured greetings are exchanged, and then utter stillness sweeps the room.

Daniel mounts the platform, turns to the audience, and begins to speak in measured tones:

"My brothers and sisters, a most extraordinary thing happened to me yesterday on the levee. For three hours I met with a man whose name is Paul—the very same Paul whose inspired letters are in our Bible. I saw for myself the brand marks of Jesus engraved on his body. There's no doubt in my mind that he is who he claims to be. In his sovereign wisdom and for his own loving purposes, God has chosen to visit this nation and speak to us tonight through his servant, Paul of Tarsus. My friends in Christ, I present to you the Apostle to the Nations."

No applause. Nary a whisper. The group is far beyond disbelief into rampant incredulity. As the apostle reaches the podium, his eyes fix on a forty-five-year-old pastor sitting in a wheelchair in the first row. A spinal injury suffered in an auto accident over a decade earlier left him paralyzed from the waist down. For the past twelve years, he hasn't taken a step.

Paul descends the stairwell, strides directly to the paralyzed man, and places a hand on his face. "In the name of Jesus Christ the Nazarene," Paul commands, "stand up and walk!"

The flummoxed pastor pushes the heels of both hands against the sides of his chair and, with a mighty effort, hoists himself erect. Almost casually, he ventures a first step and then a second—and then another and another and another. He starts to skip, suddenly runs down the center aisle, circles the entire ballroom, returns front and center, grabs the hand of his ecstatic wife, and pleads, "May I have this dance?"

Amid gasps and soft cries of "Oh, my God!" Paul returns to the podium. "I am Paul," he announces, "a slave of Jesus Christ sent on special mission to share the Word of the living God with you.

"Yesterday, Daniel shared with me an incisive appraisal of the spiritual condition among American Christians. This morning I stopped at McDonald's for an Egg McMuffin and this afternoon at Burger King for a Whopper. The fast-food culture of this country is an apt metaphor for the state of the church. You're overfed and undernourished, both physically and spiritually.

"However, there's no time to waste on jeremiads and prophecies of doom. Nor is it appropriate to pillory pastors who, like each of you, are earthen vessels with feet of clay. You must forget past failures and press on toward what lies ahead in Christ Jesus. You're living in the 'isness of the shall be,' and in this interim period of salvation-history, there's much to be done.

"First, the passionate, pursuing love of God must be proclaimed in season and out of season. Forceful emphasis must be placed on the tenderness and mercy of God, who first loved us. Instead of a light volley of divine love followed by the heavy artillery of rule-keeping, Jesus' love for the unlovely must pierce the heart of every Christian. The intellectual cognition and the experiential awareness of God are inseparable. Henceforth, the primary pastoral task is the quality of faith within the community. Every disciple can and will come to know Jesus through the baptism of fire. No other priority takes precedence; nothing else matters. The greatest part of the time, energy, talent, and financial resources of each local church is to be invested in this enterprise. Other ministries and projects will flourish as a direct result.

"Next, fraternal love will be the sign par excellence that Christians have actually experienced the love of God. Resting safe and secure in the tender compassion of the Lord, Christians will feel no need to pander to the approval and acceptance of others. Cordial love filled with respect for the sacredness of human life must be your badge of discipleship. Wrangling, bickering, and back-biting signal the loss of conscious contact with Jesus. All of you must quickly repent, ask forgiveness, and waste no time on self-recrimination.

"Authentic religion demands moderation in all things except love. The gospel tolerates a moderate love between Christians no more than it tolerates a moderate love between God and you. As I wrote to the Romans, the one who loves his or her neighbor has fulfilled the entire law of Christ and the prophets as well.

"Third and last, I want the American church to go underground for the next decade. Specifically, I urge you to return to an ancient practice of the apostolic church—the discipline of the secret. Maintain a tactful silence in the presence of unbelievers. Cultural conditioning has rendered much of your Christian language meaningless. When the latest perfume bears the name Grace—well . . . you get my point, brothers and sisters.

"As the local church lowers its profile, let it raise the bar for membership. Every disciple, no matter how mature, must have a mentor. A Christian is always in the process of becoming one. Weekly small-group meetings aren't an option solely for the devout; they're a universal necessity. Those walking the Way can't survive without support. The loner is a liar. Doubting Thomas didn't meet the risen Jesus alone in the woods but when he returned to the community of faith.

"At the dawn of the twenty-first century, it's become too easy to be a Christian. Numerically, your churches will shrink if you follow my recommendations, because as seekers old and new weigh the cost of discipleship, many will find it excessive. Don't be alarmed: Growth will develop slowly from inside out, as seekers' hearts are touched by hidden acts of unpretentious mercy. Your faithfulness will be measured by your willingness to go where there's brokenness, loneliness, and human need. What are you to draw from the life of the Master? The knowledge that love and mercy are the most powerful forces on earth.

"The discipline of the secret will disentangle the church from all the cultural accretions, devotional deviations, and religious baggage of the past. Fierce loyalty to Jesus Christ and the witness of fierce mercy to sinners will restore credibility to the Christian claim. Only he who believes is obedient, and only she who is obedient believes. Success in ministry, along with knowledge of Scripture and mastery of biblical principles, must never be confused with true discipleship. These superficial signs of faith may be the corruption of discipleship, if your life isn't hidden with Christ in God.

"Dear brothers and sisters, revive the drooping spirits of your people. Banish all anxiety and fear. Remind the saints that the crucified One, reigning in glory, has prevailed over every principality, power, and dominion. He has disarmed them, made a spectacle of them, discarded them like garments, and led them captive in his victory procession.

"With the signature of Jesus branded on my body, I, Paul, servant of the Messiah, kneel before the Father, and I pray that out of his infinite glory, he may give you the power to help your hidden self grow strong, that Christ may live in your heart through faith. And I ask him that, with both feet planted firmly on love, you'll be able to take in with all Christians the extravagant dimensions of Christ's love. Reach out and experience the breadth! Test its length! Plumb its depths! Rise to the heights! Live full lives—full in the fullness of God!"

Dear Reader,

Perhaps you will dismiss this exercise in Christian imagination as the dangerous rambling of a self-styled prophet, or perhaps you will conclude that

it has sketched accurate images of yourself and
the church of your experience. If the former, let it
go; if the latter, let it be!

Recommended Reading

Kelly, Geoffrey. *Liberating Faith.* Minneapolis: Augsburg,
 1984. This book offers a fuller development of the discipline of the secret.

Manning, Brennan. *The Signature of Jesus.* Sisters, OR:
 Multnomah Books, 1996.